PRAYING
the
GOSPELS

WITH
FR. MITCH PACWA, SJ

Jesus' Miracles in Galilee

PRAYING
the
GOSPELS

WITH
FR. MITCH PACWA, SJ

Jesus' Miracles in Galilee

the**WORD**
among us®
press

Published by The Word Among Us Press
7115 Guilford Drive, Suite 100
Frederick, Maryland 21704
www.wau.org

20 19 18 17 16   1 2 3 4 5

ISBN: 978-1-59325-288-5
eISBN: 978-1-59325-476-6

Imprimi potest: V. Rev. Brian G Paulson, SJ
Chicago-Detroit Province of the Society of Jesus
December 2, 2015

Cover design by Koechel Peterson & Associates
Cover icon of "Christ the Healer" © Monastery Icons.
Used with permission.

Made and printed in the United States of America

Library of Congress Control Number: 2016931974

Contents

Introduction

The first book of this series, *Jesus Launches His Ministry*, was an invitation to meditate on the very beginnings of Jesus' public ministry. This book will draw us into points of reflection on the various miracles of Jesus during his mission in Galilee. These miracles were the events that raised awareness of Jesus, and they were a very important reason that the people of Galilee and the surrounding districts paid attention to his teachings. So we would do well to let our attention move to Jesus' powerful deeds and become amazed at him all over again, even as the crowds were amazed.

The goal of *Jesus' Miracles in Galilee*, as with all the books in this series, is to spend time reflecting on the life of Christ so as to get to know him better. The meditations here are similar to those one might choose to consider in the Second Week of the Spiritual Exercises of St. Ignatius of Loyola. Because we need to savor the Gospel texts, I have purposely limited the number of verses in each meditation. Each chapter deals with a specific Gospel event, and each event is broken into shorter passages that are the subject of the meditation. Sometimes I use the same verse for more than one meditation in order to reflect on all its implications.

After the verses are a few paragraphs describing some of the background of the text—from the geography and scenery to the Jewish customs and ideas that lie behind the event. These are meant to help situate the events of Jesus' life and aid the imagination in entering the scenes. Jesus lived in a Middle Eastern society of two thousand years ago. The customs and language may be strange to modern people, so it is useful to try to understand these ancient ways of life and thought. However, the other goal is to see that through these cultural differences shines the humanity common to us all. The specific words and customs may differ from the modern world's ideas and expressions, but we can discover connections with the deeper truths of humanity once we better understand the context. This may help us relate our own experiences to those of the people in these stories and then discover important elements about our own relationship with Jesus Christ.

As we will see, Jesus' many miraculous actions raised important questions among the witnesses. Some people came to believe in him and some rejected him and made themselves his enemies. However, neither group denied the reality of the miracles. Even at Jesus' trials before the Sanhedrin, Herod, and Pilate, no one called his miracles fraudulent; his opponents simply feared his power, rejected his authority, and came to hate him and plot his death.

This volume ends on a somewhat disconcerting note: the Pharisees' rejection of Jesus and the disciples' incomprehension and lack of understanding of Jesus. However, keep in mind that this prepares the reader of the Gospels for the next stage of Jesus public ministry: the journey from Galilee to Jerusalem. It will begin and end with the healings of two blind men, with many teachings being directed to the disciples in between the two miracles of opening the eyes of the blind. That will be the subject of the next volume in this series.

As we enter into the meaning of the stories of the actions and miracles of Jesus, we will discover that neither the religious leaders nor his own disciples understood him. Every Christian needs to grow and develop, working through some glimmers of insight as well as through the darkness of not understanding Jesus fully. Since the disciples, who witnessed and took personal roles in so many miracles, still experienced great difficulty in knowing Jesus deeply, we can take heart and enter the journey of discovering Jesus more deeply at every stage of our Christian life.

May a deepening understanding of Jesus' miracles in this volume open our hearts to understand his teachings and accept his authority to teach radically important truths about God, human life, and our relationships with one another. May our meditations evoke good questions in our minds and hearts, and may we come to deeper faith in him as a result of our prayerful reflections.

Fr. Mitch Pacwa, SJ

CHAPTER 1

Jesus Begins His Preaching Mission throughout Galilee

LUKE 4:42-44

Jesus Begins with Private Prayer

And when it was day he departed and went into a lonely place.
(Luke 4:42a)

This short passage marks the transition from Jesus' initial ministry in Capernaum to the wider ministry throughout the region of Galilee, especially the area close to the Sea of Galilee. St. Luke begins with Jesus going away from the other people to be alone.

While St. Mark explicitly says that Jesus went out and prayed (1:35), here St. Luke only implies it, even though he, more than the other Evangelists, speaks of times when Jesus goes out alone for private prayer:

In these days he went out to the hills to pray; and all night he continued in prayer to God. And when it was day, he called his disciples, and chose from them twelve, whom he named apostles. (Luke 6:12-13)

Now it happened that as he was praying alone the disciples were with him; and he asked them, "Who do the people say that I am?" (Luke 9:18)

Now about eight days after these sayings he took with him Peter and John and James, and went up on the mountain to pray. (Luke 9:28)

He was praying in a certain place, and when he ceased, one of his disciples said to him, "Lord, teach us to pray, as John taught his disciples." (Luke 11:1)

And he withdrew from them about a stone's throw, and knelt down and prayed, "Father, if thou art willing, remove this cup from me; nevertheless not my will, but thine, be done." (Luke 22:41-42)

Each of these episodes of Jesus' private prayer leads to consequences for his disciples. In Luke 6:12-13, twelve disciples are singled out as apostles. In 9:18, the disciples are questioned about his identity until Peter confesses that Jesus is the Christ. In 9:28, three disciples climb the high mountain to see him transfigured. In 11:1 and the verses that follow, the disciples are taught how to pray to our Father in heaven. In 22:40-45, the disciples are asked to stay awake with Jesus in Gethsemane until he is arrested.

Here in Luke 4:42, Jesus prays about the next stage of his mission. His various successes in Capernaum—the exorcism in the synagogue, the healing of Peter's mother-in-law, and the large crowds coming to the house for healings—do not mean that he is to remain there permanently. His mission is not to enjoy success and build up a reputation in one town but rather to leave Capernaum and preach to all the other towns of Galilee. This time of prayer will have consequences for his disciples: will they join him or will they remain behind? Will they follow his lead or will they try to tempt him to enjoy the present successes?

Throughout life, each disciple finds it necessary to remain open to leaving behind the present success in one's life mission so as to take on the next set of tasks. The wonderful goal of making friends, finishing an education, and starting a career in early adulthood needs to give way to the vocation the Lord has in store for us—such as getting married, starting a family, or entering religious life. In our middle-aged years, as more free time becomes available and as careers change or lead to retirement, new possibilities open up for other forms of service. Jesus shows us here that we need to step away from the daily pattern of work so as to pray and seek God's will and the strength to do it.

Speak to Jesus about the last time you were faced with leaving one mission behind to take up another. Did you pray about it when the opportunity presented itself? How have you prayed through decisions facing you in the past? How did the Lord lead you? What new changes in your life might you be facing that will require prayer and discernment? Ask Jesus to guide you in making those decisions.

Conclude with an Our Father.

_____

_____

_____

_____

_____

_____

_____

_____

_____

_____

_____

MEDITATION 2

People Search for Jesus

And the people sought him and came to him, and would have kept him from leaving them. (Luke 4:42b)

Jesus' private prayer is his time of solitude with his heavenly Father, a fullness that draws him to the next stage of his mission to redeem the world. However, "the people" feel Jesus' absence. St. Luke describes them only as "the people," not as "disciples," because they have not yet made a commitment to Jesus. They have not yet made the transition from carrying on their daily lives as simple hearers and observers of Jesus' good deeds to disciples whose lives derive their meaning from following their teacher and learning everything he has to teach them.

Luke implies that the desire of the people to keep Jesus from leaving his initial successes in Capernaum was a selfish one. They had a good thing going: the demon possessed were freed and the sick and infirm were restored to health. If Jesus had remained with them, he would have been the source of miracles that would take care of their many other needs. Of course, they might also have a lurking desire to have other people hear about these miracles and come to Capernaum. Not only would the city become famous, but the economy of Capernaum would improve as the crowds of strangers arrived to meet Jesus and buy food and other supplies. The people's desire to keep Jesus in Capernaum probably included a variety of motives, such as gratitude for his good deeds, a true growing affection for him, and concerns oriented toward their own worries, needs, and wants.

This part of the episode can motivate a good examination of conscience regarding our desires and motives during various transitions in our vocations. Do we cling to our most recent successes? Do we fear leaving the recent success or satisfaction? Do we try to maintain control over our lives or gain benefits for self-centered reasons? Do we let our Lord Jesus lead us to the next stage of the Father's will for us here on earth with confidence that it will lead us to heaven as the most important goal of anything we do?

Talk to the Lord about these things. What does he say to you? What does he show you about your desires and motivations? Do you need to repent of anything?

Conclude with an Our Father.

_____

_____

_____

_____

_____

_____

_____

_____

_____

_____

_____

_____

MEDITATION 3

Jesus Clarifies His Mission
to the People

But he said to them, "I must preach the good news of the kingdom of God to the other cities also; for I was sent for this purpose." And he was preaching in the synagogues of Judea. (Luke 4:43-44)

Jesus had a clear sense of purpose in his life, a purpose given to him by the Father who sent him. He speaks about this purpose, not only in this passage, but throughout the Gospels. For instance, Jesus states that doing the Father's will is his food: "My food is to do the will of him who sent me, and to accomplish his work" (John 4:34). Seeking the Father's will rather than his own is a nourishment that sustains him like daily bread.

Furthermore, the Father's will enables him to keep moving to the next stage of the mission, and it is his guiding principle: "I seek not my own will but the will of him who sent me" (John 5:30). Neither his human will nor the will of the people in Capernaum or the rest of the world possesses the breadth of vision that the Father's will offers.

This will be the case all the way to the end of his mission, as we see in Gethsemane: "Jesus said to Peter, 'Put your sword into its sheath; shall I not drink the cup which the Father has given me?'" (John 18:11). Even his suffering and death fit within the Father's will, not because the Father enjoys Jesus' suffering, but because he can bring about his eternal glory even through igno-miny, suffering, and death.

And what is the goal of the Father's will for Jesus? Here is how he expresses it:

> "For I have come down from heaven, not to do my own will, but the will of him who sent me; and this is the will of him who sent me, that I should lose nothing of all that he has given me, but raise it up at the last day. For this is the will of my Father, that every one who sees the Son and believes in him should have eternal life; and I will raise him up at the last day." (John 6:38-40)

Ultimately, the goal of the Father's will is the redemption of every human being. God "desires all men to be saved and come to the knowledge of the truth" (1 Timothy 2:4). This will require faith in the Son, who has the power to raise up believers from the dead (John 6:40). For people to receive this faith, they will need to "see" Jesus and hear the gospel that Jesus offers them:

> But how are men to call upon him in whom they have not believed? And how are they to believe in him of whom they have never heard? And how are they to hear without a preacher? And how can men preach unless they are sent? (Romans 10:14-15)

Being "sent" applies first of all to Jesus, who must follow the Father's will and go throughout Galilee preaching the good news of the coming of the kingdom of God, with its need for repentance and faith (Matthew 4:17; Mark 1:15). As his mission progresses, he will send the disciples out to preach this same message during his public ministry (Matthew 10:7-8; Luke 9:2; 10:9-11) and after his resurrection and ascension (Acts 1:7-8).

We can reflect on how this passage is already teaching us some of the basic elements of the Lord's Prayer. Yet before teaching us to pray that the Father's will be done here on earth as in heaven, Jesus demonstrates his own determination to do the Father's will rather than his own or the will of the people around him. Before teaching us to ask the Father for our daily bread, he teaches us that doing the will of the Father is his food.

How well are we following the will of the Father? Is it our daily nourishment? Do we seek to follow God's will even when others misunderstand us or think we should be doing something different? Ask Jesus for a clear sense of purpose in your life so that you might be able to do God's will. Then, in light of Luke 4:43-44, pray the Our Father.

CHAPTER 2

The Cleansing of the Leper

MARK 1:40-45

A Leper Approaches Jesus

And a leper came to him beseeching him, and kneeling said to him,
"If you will, you can make me clean." (Mark 1:40)

The first event after Jesus moves on from Capernaum to continue his mission to the rest of Galilee is the cure of a leper.

The afflicted man takes the initiative to approach Jesus and pleads with him to make him "clean." The leper says, "If you will" (*theles*), indicating his recognition that Jesus can accomplish whatever he wills to do, even something as seemingly impossible as curing such as disease. Leprosy, which today is known as Hansen's Disease, was brought to the Mediterranean world in the fourth century BC by the armies of Alexander the Great upon their return from an invasion of India. The ancients knew of no way to cure this horrible disease, which took a person's life by rotting their limbs and appendages. Lepers were considered to be the "walking dead," and isolating them was the only means of preventing the spread of the disease. Lepers were forced to live apart from the rest of society as they endured pain, the loss of limbs, increasing disability, and inevitable death.

In addition to being sick with an incurable deadly disease, those with leprosy were considered to be ritually unclean and thereby unable to worship in the Temple or synagogue. As the disease progressed, pieces of their skin and bones would fall off, evidence of decay and impending death. Since the God of Israel is a God "of the living" (Matthew 22:32; Mark 12:27; Luke

20:38), lepers, "the walking dead," would bring the decay of death inside the Temple or the synagogues and so were not permitted to worship God with the rest of the community. Not only did other people fear contagion through contact with lepers, but they also wanted to avoid the ritual uncleanness that automatically was passed on to anyone who had touched them.

What can we learn from this leper? Hansen's Disease is not the only reason people become isolated from one another. Some, particularly those who are young, do not know how to find a group that accepts them. Some isolate themselves for physical reasons—perhaps they feel unattractive or overweight. Those who are poor may feel out of place because of what they are wearing or where they live. Members of ethnic or racial minorities, people confused about their sexual identity, and many other people isolate themselves, usually in response to subtle or not so subtle signals from their society. In fact, most people feel isolated from others at some time in their lives.

The response to isolation can range from self-pity to rage, from self-inflicted wounds and suicide to lashing out at others and violence. This leper may have gone through those experiences during his life, but at this point he is in the Gospel only because he reached out to Jesus, humbly knelt before him, and made an act of faith: "If you will, you can make me clean."

Think back on the times you have felt isolated. How did you handle it? How did you understand the problem that caused the isolation, and what did you do about it? Even if it was many years ago, it is worth remembering. Picture Jesus entering those times of isolation and social "leprosy." What would you say to him now? How might he respond to you now?

Conclude this meditation with the prayer Soul of Christ (*Anima Christi*; see appendix).

Jesus Responds to the Leper

Moved with pity, he stretched out his hand and touched him, and said to him, "I will; be clean." And immediately the leprosy left him, and he was made clean. (Mark 1:41-42)

Jesus responds to the leper in three ways: with emotion, with a loving touch, and with a healing act of the will.

First, Jesus is "moved with pity," a passive participle of a verb derived from a noun, *splanchna*, meaning "the inner organs"—heart, lungs, liver, kidneys, and spleen. The Greek translation of the Old Testament uses it for the same organs, but with the Hebrew sense, as the seat of emotions. The later Jewish literature develops the verb form to mean "to feel compassion or pity." Jesus uses this verb to describe the compassion of the father when he sees his prodigal son return (Luke 15:20) as well as the Good Samaritan who truly loves his neighbor (Luke 10:33) and the king who forgives the servant's enormous debt (Matthew 18:23.) All other uses of the verb in the Gospels apply only to Jesus, who regularly shows compassion. (In Matthew 9:36, 14:14, and 15:32, Jesus shows compassion for the weary crowds, and in 20:34, he shows compassion as he heals two blind men).

Second, Jesus "stretched out his hand and touched him" (Mark 1:41), an action that was forbidden because of the leper's contagion. Touching a leper entailed two risks: first, a person could contract the disease through contact with the virus; and second, the person would certainly become ritually unclean and could not participate at the Temple or synagogue until having taken a ritual bath in a *mikvah*. Yet Jesus' touch expressed his compassion in a concrete way, just as when he touched the eyes of the blind men out of compassion and healed them both (Matthew 20:34).

Third, Jesus says, "I will" (*thelo*), not in the English sense of acting in the future, but instead of making an act of the will. Then he adds, "Be clean" (Mark 1:41). The leprosy left the man and he was cured "immediately" (1:42). Jesus' compassion reached out, his touch expressed his love for an untouchable man, and his act of the will and his word were immediately effective in re-creating a man who had been doomed to die.

Jesus' three actions—welling up with compassion, touching the physically and ritually unclean leper, and drawing down from the depths of his will to heal the man—demonstrate his full humanity and his full divinity. Because of his human nature, he can touch and feel compassion; because of his divinity, he can will to heal and make it happen. Throughout his ministry of performing miracles, both of his natures cooperated in complete harmony.

As we contemplate each miracle, let us enter into the same sense of wonder that the crowds originally experienced. Picture the events as vividly as possible and marvel at the mystery of the fullness of Jesus' divinity operating in his humanity, neither nature rejected or forsaken but both acting together for the salvation of various individuals in various ways. Of course, Jesus will confound some observers. Our salvation flows from humbly accepting all aspects of the mystery of Jesus without denying him in any way.

Conclude these reflections with an Our Father.

_____

_____

_____

_____

_____

_____

_____

_____

_____

_____

_____

_____

_____

_____

_____

_____

_____

_____

_____

_____

_____

Jesus, the Physician of Our Souls

And immediately the leprosy left him, and he was made clean.
(Mark 1:42)

In the Maronite Rite, the Second Sunday of Great Lent is known as "the Sunday of the Leper." One prayer in that liturgy addresses Jesus, who "appeared in the world as a physician and granted the sick wholeness of body and soul" and asks the Lord, "O Christ our God, Physician of souls and bodies, . . . look upon us and have compassion, as you had compassion on the man with leprosy. Come to us, cleanse us, and make us whole." Though very few people in the West suffer from leprosy, it is true that everywhere in the world and in every period of history, "all have sinned and fall short of the glory of God" (Romans 3:23). Therefore, sin can be compared to leprosy because it distorts our human nature and diminishes the dignity inherent in each person, who is made in the image and likeness of God (see Genesis 1:26-27). For that reason, each person needs Jesus to forgive their sins and cleanse their consciences.

In light of this leper, we would do well to consider the ways in which sin may have become a deadly pattern in our own lives. Perhaps we struggle with alcohol or drug abuse, which not only damages or destroys brain cells, the liver, and other physical organs but also deadens the soul and destroys interpersonal relationships. Perhaps by separating sex from authentic love and marriage, our relationships have become destructive. Lustful use and abuse of another person is the basis for patterns of sin that isolate us from God and from each other. Perhaps we struggle with anger, narcissism, pride, materialism, or something else. We each need to reflect on our own sins in order to identify the leprous qualities that isolate us from the true love of others, keep us from loving and worshipping God, and doom us to death in this world and spiritual death in eternity.

From this perspective, we each can picture ourselves approaching Jesus as the leper did: "If you will, you can heal me." We can be absolutely sure that Jesus wants to heal not only our sinful deeds but also the effects of those sins on our personal, social, and religious lives. Jesus will well up with compassion for our predicaments, reach out to touch the depths of our hearts, and choose to make us whole if we approach him with trusting faith.

Conclude with an Our Father.

Death Is God's Enemy

And he sternly charged him, and sent him away at once. (Mark 1:43)

Jesus took this healing very seriously, as seen by the phrase "sternly charged" (which translates a single Greek word) and the rather harsh "sent him away at once." The force of Jesus' reaction leads some scholars to compare this healing to an exorcism in which an evil spirit is expelled. However, Jesus' reaction to the healing of the leper, a man who had been counted among the "walking dead," may be better understood in light of the scriptural teaching that death is God's enemy.

God did not make death, / and he does not delight in the death of the living. / For he created all things that they might exist, / and the generative forces of the world are wholesome, / and there is no destructive poison in them; / and the dominion of Hades is not on earth. / For righteousness is immortal. / But ungodly men by their words and deeds summoned death; / considering him a friend, they pined away, / and they made a covenant with him, / because they are fit to belong to his party. (Wisdom 1:13-16)

For he must reign until he has put all his enemies under his feet. The last enemy to be destroyed is death. (1 Corinthians 15:25-26)

"O death, where is thy victory? / O death, where is thy sting?" / The sting of death is sin, and the power of sin is the law. But thanks be to God, who gives us the victory through our Lord Jesus Christ. (1 Corinthians 15:55-57)

Death is an enemy that Christ came to defeat, along with the unclean spirits, as he introduced the kingdom of God into the world. Therefore, when he confronts leprosy, the death that gradually overpowers the afflicted person, Jesus reacts with great vigor and even anger.

We would do well to consider Jesus' stern charge in light of God's enmity with death. The last century was the most violent in human history: 305 million people died in wars of nationalism or the atheistic oppression of Communism. In addition, hundreds of millions of abortions have taken place, and suicide has in some places been legalized and renamed "euthanasia" (Greek for "happy death"). In many situations, the secular culture rejects the place of God and allies itself with God's enemy, death.

What is our own attitude? How stern are we in opposing death as a solution to the world's problems, which results in war, abortion, euthanasia, and other sins against humanity? Do we send it away from us "at once"? Do we cling to Jesus Christ, who personifies "the resurrection and the life" (John 11:25)? Do we bring the new life that Jesus has to offer to those who desperately need it? What might God be calling you to do to defeat the culture of death?

Conclude with an Our Father.

MEDITATION 5

The Cleansing

[Jesus] said to him, "See that you say nothing to any one; but go, show yourself to the priest, and offer for your cleansing what Moses commanded, for a proof to the people." But he went out and began to talk freely about it, and to spread the news, so that Jesus could no longer openly enter a town, but was out in the country; and people came to him from every quarter. (Mark 1:44-45)

First, Jesus orders the man to keep quiet about the miracle, not unlike his command that silenced the demon-possessed man in the synagogue (Luke 4:35). Jesus had ordered various demons not to announce his identity, not because their information was false, but because he did not want them to say it. Repeatedly Jesus silences both people he has healed and the disciples about his identity. Yet while Jesus was on the cross, the centurion proclaims, "Truly this man was the Son of God!" (Mark 15:39). Only in Jesus' death on the cross can we understand the meaning of the incarnation of God the Son. The miracles give important evidence, but his death and resurrection are the true keys to understanding Jesus' identity, and neither the devils nor the cleansed leper can reveal that truth.

Next, Jesus instructs the cured leper to show himself to the priest and then offer sacrifice. This mention of the sacrifice commanded by the Lord through Moses can be understood only if we examine the text of Leviticus 14. The sacrifice was a ritual lasting eight days. Someone with a skin disease needed to be examined by the priest to affirm that it was gone. This was followed by an initial sacrifice and cleansing ceremony with two birds, one of which was set free as a symbol of freedom from the disease, while the other was sacrificed as a sign of the deadliness of the disease. The person cleansed himself, even to the point of shaving all his body hair, and washed his clothes as a thorough purification. The seven-day waiting period proved that he was completely healed and not merely in remission. On the seventh day, he washed again in preparation for the eighth-day sacrifices. These included a guilt offering, cleansing by anointing himself with the blood of a lamb, and an atonement offering of the lamb, grain, and oil.

Certainly, Christians do not have to offer these sacrifices because Jesus Christ is our High Priest who offers himself. He is the Lamb of God who is sacrificed as a self-gift rather than as an offering of some other object. Therefore, we are washed in his blood, as Scripture tells us:

> They have washed their robes and made them white in the blood of the Lamb. (Revelation 7:14)

> How much more shall the blood of Christ, who through the eternal Spirit offered himself without blemish to God, purify your conscience from dead works to serve the living God. Therefore he is the mediator of a new covenant. (Hebrews 9:14-15)

> The blood of Jesus his Son cleanses us from all sin. (1 John 1:7)

Jesus' blood, therefore, replaces being cleansed by the blood of a lamb. Christians experience the power of Jesus cleansing them from sin in Baptism:

But you were washed, you were sanctified, you were justified in the name of the Lord Jesus Christ and in the Spirit of our God. (1 Corinthians 6:11)

Christ loved the church and gave himself up for her, that he might sanctify her, having cleansed her by the washing of water with the word, that he might present the church to himself in splendor, without spot or wrinkle or any such thing, that she might be holy and without blemish. (Ephesians 5:25-27)

The washing in Baptism replaces the washing of a leper in a bath (Leviticus 14:8) by a washing that cleanses the soul of original sin or any other sin committed before Baptism. For sins committed after Baptism, the Sacrament of Confession, or Reconciliation, cleanses the soul. Instead of examining the body for physical leprosy, a person examines his conscience and heart in order to know and admit to any and all sins. The goal is forgiveness by Jesus Christ and a change of life as radical as the cleansing of the leper.

Part of the purpose of the ceremony of cleansing a leper is the restoration of the leper to the community of worship, symbolized in the eighth-day sacrifices. So also, Confession restores a person to a worthy reception of Holy Communion and a share in the sacrifice of the Mass and the other sacraments.

Reflect on God's mercy, that he has provided a way for you to be cleansed of your sin through the blood of Jesus. How often do you thank Jesus for shedding his blood to save you? Do you carry that sense of gratitude with you throughout your day or week? Do you take advantage of the cleansing you can receive in Confession? How "clean" do you feel when you leave the confessional?

The final verse of this passage shows the leper's disobedience to Christ's stern command to him. The former leper was so overjoyed by his healing that he told everyone about it. However, his disobedience interfered with Jesus' mission by making it difficult for Jesus to enter towns. This new obstacle was not insurmountable, as witnessed by the people coming out to the countryside to see him, but it brings out the point that human disobedience has consequences not foreseen by its perpetrators. This helps remind us to obey God, even when we do not see the consequences ourselves. Ask yourself, "Do I trust in God enough to obey his commands, even when I don't foresee all the consequences of my disobedience?"

Conclude with the prayer the Soul of Christ.

CHAPTER 3

The Healing of a Paralytic

MARK 2:1-12

The Reaction to Jesus' Return to Capernaum

And when he returned to Capernaum after some days, it was reported that he was at home. And many were gathered together, so that there was no longer room for them, not even about the door; and he was preaching the word to them. (Mark 2:1-2)

Most probably, Jesus' preaching tour centered around the Sea of Galilee, especially in the nearby towns and villages such as Chorazin and Bethsaida. Upon his return to Capernaum, a large crowd had gathered around the house of Simon and his mother-in-law, desiring to hear Jesus teach them "the word" (Mark 2:2). Before he left town, they had focused on bringing him their sick and demon possessed (1:32-34), but in his absence their hunger for his teaching had grown. Perhaps his absence was necessary to awaken their desire for his more profound gift of the word of God, the teaching that offers meaning for the whole of existence, including life after death.

People develop in stages: beginning as infants, we become toddlers, then children and adolescents, and finally we move into the various stages of adulthood. Each stage has a purpose or set of goals, with the earlier stages establishing the foundations for the later stages. For instance, toddlers learn to walk and talk, skills that serve them throughout their lives. Our faith also develops in stages throughout our lives. In the earliest stages, we learn to pray for the people we love and eventually for the things we want from God. We typically go through crises of faith when

God does not answer our prayers as we desire or when we question what was taught us by our parents.

Like the people of Capernaum, we need to go through times when the Lord seems absent, no longer doing the things we asked for when we ask or how we ask. Like them, we need to learn to seek his deeper, more mature gifts, in this case, his teaching rather than easy health care. We would do well to examine some of those times when we have experienced disappointment in our relationship with God, or even disillusionment. Did we welcome the Lord's reappearance in our lives with openness to meeting him on his terms? Did we accept the next stage in our relationship with him?

Conclude with an Our Father.

_____

_____

_____

_____

_____

_____

_____

_____

_____

_____

_____

_____

_____

Friends Carry the Paralytic to Jesus

The four men carrying their paralyzed friend had not completely forgotten Jesus' ability to heal:

And they came, bringing to him a paralytic carried by four men. And when they could not get near him because of the crowd, they removed the roof above him; and when they had made an opening, they let down the pallet on which the paralytic lay. (Mark 2:3-4)

The four friends climb the roof and make an opening large enough for them to lower the pallet holding the paralyzed man. They are not satisfied to keep him on the edge of the large crowd outside the house but insist that he be placed with those gathered inside, close to Jesus. The paralytic's bond of kinship or friendship with the four strong men gives them both energy and ingenuity, though not a strong respect for Peter's roof. They lift him up to the top of the house, remove the straw and mud thatch from the roof, and let him down by ropes into the middle of the already overly crowded house.

And when Jesus saw their faith, he said to the paralytic, "My son, your sins are forgiven." (Mark 2:5)

Jesus reads their loving action for a paralyzed man as an expression of faith. Instead of a formal statement of faith, their clever act of loving devotion to bring their friend close to Jesus is taken by Jesus as an indication of their faith.

Recognizing their faith leads Jesus to speak a word of forgiveness of the paralytic's sins. Were the disabled man and the four friends looking for forgiveness at that moment? Obviously they sought a physical healing; that was the need that appeared most evident to them. They had not come in sackcloth and ashes; they had not asked for the forgiveness of sins. No one had even mentioned sin. Yet that is what Jesus offers the man.

How often do we seek a particular need or want, but something unsought is given to us? When I was twelve, my grandmother assured me that I was going to love my Christmas present from her. I thought I was getting the HO-gauge electric train engine that I really wanted. I opened up a too-small package to find a silver miraculous medal. Though I tried to act as happy as she had promised I would be, I was not. However, that was just around the time that I stopped playing with HO trains, and I still have that miraculous medal.

Jesus knows the deeper, truer needs that lie below the desires that we know how to express. In this case, forgiveness of sin effected the reconciliation with God and the personal integrity that could satisfy the paralyzed man better than the ability to walk. One day he would die, unable to walk ever again. The forgiveness of sins brought integrity and peace at that moment, and it could accompany him into an eternity beyond the need for legs for transport.

When have you asked the Lord for something you really wanted but did not receive? What did the Lord give you instead? Were you later able to see that it was a better gift? Are you still waiting to see God's plan behind the gift that he did give to you? Ask the Lord to show you his greater plan for your life. What might you be asking for now that you are not receiving from the Lord? What other gift might the Lord be offering you?

Conclude with an Our Father.

_____

_____

_____

_____

_____

_____

_____

_____

_____

_____

_____

_____

_____

_____

_____

_____

_____

_____

_____

_____

_____

MEDITATION 3

Who Has the Authority
to Forgive Sins?

Now some of the scribes were sitting there, questioning in their
hearts, "Why does this man speak thus? It is blasphemy! Who
can forgive sins but God alone?" (Mark 2:6-7)

The scribes, who were the scholars within the party of
the Pharisees, reacted to Jesus' offer of forgiveness of
sins not with faith but with a critical questioning. They
posed their question about Jesus within their hearts; they did
not speak directly to him so as to confront him or be confronted
by him. Rather, they answered their own question by assuming
that Jesus had committed blasphemy, based on their theological
principle that only God could forgive sins, since God is the one
offended by sin.

And immediately Jesus, perceiving in his spirit that they thus
questioned within themselves, said to them, "Why do you question thus in your hearts? Which is easier, to say to the paralytic,
'Your sins are forgiven,' or to say, 'Rise, take up your pallet and
walk'? But that you may know that the Son of man has authority
on earth to forgive sins"—he said to the paralytic—"I say to you,
rise, take up your pallet and go home." (Mark 2:8-11)

The scribes' doubts give rise to two kinds of evidence for
Jesus' divinity and therefore for his authority to forgive sins.
First, Jesus knows the inner thoughts of the scribes. Such

knowledge of another person's heart and mind is the preroga-
tive of God, as the Old Testament regularly affirmed:

> For the LORD sees not as man sees; man looks on the outward
> appearance, but the LORD looks on the heart. (1 Samuel 16:7)

> You know when I sit down and when I rise up; / you discern my
> thoughts from afar. (Psalm 139:2)

> The LORD searches all hearts, and understands every plan and
> thought. (1 Chronicles 28:9)

The New Testament applies this same principle to Jesus:

> Jesus did not trust himself to them, because he knew all men and
> needed no one to bear witness of man; for he himself knew what
> was in man. (John 2:24-25)

> And before him no creature is hidden, but all are open and laid
> bare to the eyes of him with whom we have to do. (Hebrews 4:13)

Since it is true that only God can know the inner thoughts
of individual people, and since Jesus demonstrates that ability
throughout the Gospels, clearly he is God. Because he is God, he
does have the authority to forgive the paralytic's sins.

The second proof of Christ's divinity is his ability to heal the
paralytic simply by speaking the command "Rise." A prophecy
given around the end of the Babylonian exile announced a new
exodus from Babylon in which even the lame could participate
because the Lord would heal them:

Strengthen the weak hands, / and make firm the feeble knees. / Say to those who are of a fearful heart, / "Be strong, fear not! / Behold, your God / will come with vengeance, / with the recompense of God. / He will come and save you." / Then the eyes of the blind shall be opened, / and the ears of the deaf unstopped; / then shall the lame man leap like a hart, / and the tongue of the dumb sing for joy. / For waters shall break forth in the wilderness, / and streams in the desert. (Isaiah 35:3-6)

The healing of the lame, the blind, and the deaf is a sign that "God will come," so Jesus' healing of the paralytic indicates that he is the God who has come to save Israel—if they will only recognize him. In this case, Jesus heals the paralytic precisely to demonstrate his divinity and therefore his power to forgive sins.

People who seek out Jesus as the paralytic and his friends did frequently find more in him than they ever expected. The expectations of the five men were high—they were looking for Jesus to heal a man who could not walk. The man received forgiveness of his sins, and the scribes and the rest of the crowd learned that Jesus could read not only the paralytic's heart and sense his deepest needs but also knew the interior thoughts of those who doubted his power. Further, Jesus was still able to heal the paralytic. In all this, Jesus was revealing new depths of who God is and the effects of his presence among us.

Are we as open to accepting the richness that Jesus reveals as he offers that richness to us? As we reflect on this question, we can pray, "Jesus, show me even more of your infinite goodness. Forgive my sins; know my heart; heal all my hurts. Jesus, I trust in you."

Conclude with an Our Father.

_____

_____

_____

_____

_____

_____

_____

_____

_____

_____

_____

_____

_____

_____

_____

_____

_____

_____

_____

Results and Reaction

And he rose, and immediately took up the pallet and went out before them all; so that they were all amazed and glorified God, saying, "We never saw anything like this!" (Mark 2:12)

The first reaction to Jesus' command to "Rise, take up your pallet" (Mark 2:9) comes from the healed paralytic. After Jesus has accomplished a healing that only God can do, the recipient of the healing does what he is now able to do: walk out of the house carrying his own pallet.

The second reaction comes from the crowd: these witnesses were "amazed" and glorified God as the proper response to a deed that no one had ever seen. They did not explicitly attribute Jesus' action to his divinity; their faith had not yet developed to that point. However, their amazement indicates the beginnings of their faith, just as the efforts and love of the four friends were the first indications of their faith at the beginning of the episode.

Look back on your life and consider the ways in which your faith in Jesus has begun to grow. How did some of your actions indicate the beginnings of that faith? What have you experienced Jesus doing in life that confirms the reality of that faith? How does greater knowledge of God's nature as revealed in Scripture help you better understand Jesus? How do the prophecies of the Old Testament clarify Jesus' identity for you? Do you experience any of the amazement about the way Jesus has worked in your life, as the crowd did? What still amazes you?

Like the crowd, glorify God and give him thanks for all he has done in your life. Offer this praise by praying Psalm 100, or the Gloria from Mass, or by simply and slowly praying the Glory Be. Perhaps even listen to the Gloria from one of the great Mass compositions: Bach's *Mass in B Minor* or Beethoven's *Missa Solemnis*. Make this your prayer of glory to God for all he has done in your life.

_____

_____

_____

_____

_____

_____

_____

_____

_____

_____

_____

_____

_____

_____

_____

_____

_____

_____

_____

CHAPTER 4

The Healing of a Man with a Withered Hand

MARK 3:1-6

The Synagogue Becomes a Battleground

Up to this point in the Gospel of Mark, the emphasis has been on Jesus' authority over demons, illness, and the law. Particularly throughout Mark 2, we see the Pharisees' growing opposition to Jesus' authority, whether in reference to forgiving sins, associating with sinners, or living the sabbath regulations. Mark 3:1-6 brings this tension to a head when a healing in a synagogue on a Sabbath moves the Pharisees and their political allies, the Herodians, to plan to kill Jesus.

> Again he entered the synagogue, and a man was there who had a withered hand. And they watched him, to see whether he would heal him on the sabbath, so that they might accuse him. And he said to the man who had the withered hand, "Come here." (Mark 3:1-3)

Jesus takes the initiative in this tense situation by commanding the man with the withered hand to "Stand up in the middle" (a more literal translation of the Greek). By commanding the man to stand so visibly at the center of the synagogue, Jesus was provoking the Pharisees, who were looking for a reason to accuse Jesus of something, and increasing the tension.

> And he said to them, "Is it lawful on the sabbath to do good or to do harm, to save life or to kill?" But they were silent. (Mark 3:4)

With the man standing in the middle of the synagogue floor, Jesus brings the attention to himself with a question based on the Pharisees' own terminology: "Is it lawful?" While Scripture prohibited work on the Sabbath, the tradition of the Pharisees placed a "fence around Torah," by defining ever more precisely the actions that were permitted on the Sabbath, even to the point of counting the number of steps one could take in between each meal.

Jesus does not start with the Pharisees' presuppositions but goes back to first principles: should the sabbath rest prevent doing the good deed of healing? Jewish law allowed medical attention to be given only if a life was in danger, but Jesus phrases the question in such a way that he puts his opponents in a quandary. No one would expect the Pharisees to say that it is right to do evil on the Sabbath, but neither would they agree to doing good if that would give Jesus permission to heal the man, which was a type of "work."

The second part of Jesus' question implies that leaving the man with a withered hand is equivalent to taking his life. Jesus uses the word "kill" rather than neglect, which indicates that the growing enmity between him and the Pharisees would provoke them to put him to death. His inevitable death will become a prominent issue even at this early stage.

Jesus is not afraid of the tension; he knows it is present and he confronts it directly. He wants the real issue of the man with a withered hand to be front and center, so that everyone knows that a real human being is at stake. He also knows that his opponents are not committed to the deeper issues of God's law or to life but primarily to themselves. As we face a culture in which many are willing to ignore the truth in order to get what they want, are we afraid? Do we want people to like us, or are we committed to the good of others? Do we have a clear understanding of the deeper truth of God's commandments, and are we able to see through arguments that twist or relativize the truth?

As you picture Jesus speaking to the crowd and to his opponents in a stone synagogue, talk to him about the source of his courage to confront his culture. Talk to to him of the times you are afraid to speak up to people who deny the truth of God's commandments or who refuse to serve life. Ask Jesus to teach you how to find the type of courage he had in the synagogue and everywhere else he went.

Conclude with the prayer the Soul of Christ.

_____

_____

_____

_____

_____

_____

_____

_____

_____

_____

_____

_____

_____

Jesus Heals the Man and His Enemies Conspire to Kill Him

And he looked around at them with anger, grieved at their hardness of heart, and said to the man, "Stretch out your hand." He stretched it out, and his hand was restored. (Mark 3:5)

Jesus is angry and frustrated at the cowardly silence of those who want to trap him. They refuse to speak up and choose whether they will "do good or do harm, save life or kill" (Mark 3:4). He is also grieved by their obstinate, hard-hearted antagonism that does not permit sympathy with a suffering man that would lead them to seek his good.

In that state of mind, Jesus gives a second command to the man with the withered hand: "Stretch out your hand" (Mark 3:5). Jesus has a pattern of asking people to do something by their own efforts after he does what only God can do (see 2:11). He wants people to cooperate with his gracious action in order to draw them into a relationship rather than merely get something from him.

The Pharisees went out, and immediately held counsel with the Herodians against him, how to destroy him. (Mark 3:6)

The Herodians (mentioned only here and in Mark 12:13) were political agents for Herod, who were sought by the Pharisees in an alliance against Jesus. In this moment, the question posed by Jesus in Mark 3:4 becomes all the more poignant: "Is it lawful on the sabbath to do good or to do harm, to save life or to kill?" The Pharisees who were so angry with Jesus for healing a man on the Sabbath now use the Sabbath to plan ways to kill and destroy him. The healing of the man's withered hand lays bare the depth of the conflict between Jesus' ever-increasing authority and his opponents' hardness of heart. It becomes a conflict between Jesus, the source of life, healing, and forgiveness, and those who plot death and destruction.

This conflict between life and death, holiness and sin, has existed throughout the ages, from Cain and Abel until the present time. Where do you see this struggle taking place today? What issues most concern you? Where do you presently stand on those issues?

Ask our Lord how he wants you to engage in these concerns. What would he expect you to do in the face of the opposition that comes against Christians from the forces of deceit, evil, and death? Speak to him, and more important, listen to him about your concerns, your inclinations, and your fears.

Conclude with the prayer the Soul of Christ.

_____

_____

_____

_____

_____

_____

_____

_____

_____

_____

_____

_____

_____

_____

_____

_____

_____

_____

_____

_____

_____

_____

_____

_____

_____

_____

_____

_____

_____

_____

_____

_____

CHAPTER 5

The Centurion's Request for a Healing

MATTHEW 8:5-13

A Centurion Approaches Jesus to Heal a Servant

As he entered Capernaum, a centurion came forward to him, beseeching him and saying, "Lord, my servant is lying paralyzed at home, in terrible distress." And he said to him, "I will come and heal him." (Matthew 8:5-7)

Jesus had recently returned from one of his journeys to the neighboring towns in Galilee. Upon entering Capernaum, he is approached by a centurion, an officer in the Roman army who commanded one hundred men. Capernaum was the last town in Herod Antipas' territory situated on the Via Maris, the road that connected the Mediterranean coast with Damascus and the rest of the Middle East. The centurion was stationed there to ensure security and the collection of taxes. Frequent caravans with rich goods passed through seeking food, fodder, and shelter as well as safety from brigands along the road.

Not many miles north, the road entered into the territory of Herod's brother Philip, who would take responsibility for safety on the road at that point. Excavations in the northern end of Capernaum have revealed a Roman bath, which indicates the presence of enough Roman soldiers in town to require an officer of the centurion rank. (Jews went to the *mikvah*, a ritual bath.)

Upon initially hearing this story, a first-century Jewish audience would not have been particularly pleased that Jesus willingly responded to the petition of a centurion, who represented the foreign occupying troops who enforced the heavy taxation of their people. However, St. Luke adds another detail to this episode:

> When he heard of Jesus, he sent to him elders of the Jews, asking him to come and heal his slave. And when they came to Jesus, they besought him earnestly, saying, "He is worthy to have you do this for him, for he loves our nation, and he built us our synagogue." (Luke 7:3-5)

When pilgrims to Capernaum visit the ancient synagogue today, they see the existing ruins, a white limestone structure, which was built in the late fourth century. However, below the limestone floor is a foundation of dark gray basalt stone from the first century, the time of Jesus, and it was that foundation, with an earlier basalt building above it, that the centurion had built for the people of Capernaum. That loving deed made the elders willing to bring his request to Jesus.

However, Jesus, who had preached from the beginning, "The kingdom of God is at hand; repent and believe" (Mark 1:15), perceived that the centurion's act of love for the people of Israel manifested a certain level of faith in the Lord God whom they worshipped within the synagogue. We might even suppose that something attracted or at least fascinated the centurion about the Jews' worship of the one God, the creator and judge of all, who possessed a moral quality that he, as a pagan, could not find among his own gods, let alone those who worshipped them. The serious way that Jews oriented their lives around pleasing the one Lord God would have seemed odd to a Roman. Yet this centurion apparently looked beyond mere cultural differences and saw a goodness and depth in the Lord God that opened his heart and mind to faith.

Consider the kind of example you are giving about the way your faith in Jesus Christ affects your life. Are you providing the kind of witness to nonbelievers that makes them wonder what makes your faith so important to you? Do they pose questions based on your way of life? If so, how do you answer them?

Consider also that some people you meet have the beginnings of faith or faith at a different level. Do you come down harshly on them for the incompleteness of their faith or understanding of morals? Or do you meet them at the level of faith and love they possess? How do you help them mature in faith?

Picture yourself in Capernaum as the centurion's petition for a healing arrives. What would you think of it? Speak to Jesus about your attitude toward unbelievers. What might he say to you about your witness to them or the way you have spoken to them? Consider Matthew's assessment of Jesus: "He will not break a bruised reed / or quench a smoldering wick" (12:20).

Conclude with the prayer the Soul of Christ.

_____

_____

_____

_____

_____

_____

_____

_____

_____

_____

_____

_____

_____

_____

_____

_____

_____

_____

_____

_____

_____

_____

_____

_____

The Centurion's Humble Faith

But the centurion answered him, "Lord, I am not worthy to have you come under my roof; but only say the word, and my servant will be healed. For I am a man under authority, with soldiers under me; and I say to one, 'Go,' and he goes, and to another, 'Come,' and he comes, and to my slave, 'Do this,' and he does it." (Matthew 8:8-9)

In the face of Jesus' willingness to come heal the servant, the centurion objects because of his awareness of being unworthy to have Jesus in his home. This profound humility is followed by an understanding of Jesus' power and authority, based on an analogy from his own experience as an officer. Clearly, this man has thought deeply about Jesus as being both holy and powerful: Jesus' holiness makes the centurion unworthy to have Jesus come to his home; Jesus' power makes it unnecessary for him to come.

The Church has been impressed by this centurion's faith for centuries, as seen in her request that in the moments immediately before the priest distributes Holy Communion, everyone professes the centurion's humble act of faith. As the priest holds up the Body of Christ before the whole congregation and announces that this is the Lamb of God who takes away the sins of the world, the priest and people respond together, "Lord, I am not worthy that you should enter under my roof, but only say the word and my soul shall be healed." Each person thereby recognizes the need for healing inside the soul because even after the confession of sin and the reception of reconciliation, its damaging effects remain. However, unlike the centurion who prevents Jesus from entering his house, we come forward to receive Jesus—Body, Blood, Soul, and Divinity—so that he can bestow a healing that permeates our souls to their very depths.

We would do well to consider the infinite holiness and power of the Person we are inviting into our hearts in Holy Communion. Some Catholics in recent decades have emphasized the Mass as a meal in which we share fellowship with other people in the church. This is a true enough perspective, but its emphasis is on human participation in Holy Communion rather than on the One who is being received. The centurion was aware, however vaguely, that Jesus was no ordinary person but someone in greater authority than he, the ranking officer representing the Roman Empire in town. He perceived that truth despite the ordinariness of Jesus' clothing and humility.

We are called to perceive the infinite Son of God present under the appearance of a very humble piece of bread. We are to be so aware of him in faith that we proclaim with St. Thomas, "My Lord and my God" (John 20:28). We believe this sacrament is no longer bread but the Body of Christ, and we say "Amen" to this act of faith as we receive Jesus "under our roof" and invite him to dwell in our hearts. Consider these points, and conclude with the prayer the Soul of Christ.

Jesus Praises the Centurion

When Jesus heard him, he marveled, and said to those who followed him, "Truly, I say to you, not even in Israel have I found such faith. I tell you, many will come from east and west and sit at table with Abraham, Isaac, and Jacob in the kingdom of heaven, while the sons of the kingdom will be thrown into the outer darkness; there men will weep and gnash their teeth." (Matthew 8:10-12)

Jesus recognized the centurion's humility as an expression of faith, a faith that exceeded that of most of the people of Israel. This added to his marvel: the Israelites had a nineteen-hundred-year experience of dealing with their relationship with God, from Abraham to the time of Jesus. They had made many serious mistakes and committed many sins, suffering from them but also learning profound lessons of faith from them, especially after the Babylonian exile. However, this Gentile expressed more faith than the Israelites around him through his humility and trust in Christ's power than they did with their far more sophisticated theological formulas.

Jesus then took the opportunity to state that many more strangers would come "from east and west" to share in the banquet of the kingdom of heaven. He foreknew that foreigners, most of whom the people of Israel had not yet even heard of, would believe in him and find salvation in the kingdom of heaven. Yet as can be seen throughout Jesus' parables, those who do not have faith will be thrown into the darkness of eternal suffering. Those who refuse to believe will endure the wordless pain that results from being separated from God.

We need to consider our own faith. Will we have faith and trust in Jesus, by which he invites us into the banquet of God's kingdom? Or will we be shut out in that great darkness in which we will be unable to find words that express the pain, as our voices wail and we gnash our teeth in despair? Will we eventually be in the position of the centurion, to whom Jesus said the following?

> And to the centurion Jesus said, "Go; be it done for you as you have believed." And the servant was healed at that very moment. (Matthew 8:13)

The centurion's humble faith made possible his servant's healing. Had he rejected faith, he would not have received his request. His unworthiness did not prevent the healing; his humble faith was the measure by which Christ made the healing possible.

Ask the Lord for a deepening of faith. Faith is a "theological virtue," which means that it is God's gift. Yet like the centurion, we also need the disposition of humility that makes it possible to trust God's truth above our own opinions. We need to ask for faith and receive the gift with a free will that chooses to take God's truth on his terms rather than our own.

Conclude with the Apostles' Creed or Nicene Creed, considering each statement of faith and assenting to it with your whole mind and heart. Make your act of faith an expression of both your love for God and for his truth.

CHAPTER 6

The Raising of the Widow of Nain's Son

LUKE 7:11-17

Jesus Shows Compassion to a Bereft Widow

The previous miracle involved saving the centurion's servant from a serious illness; here Jesus raises a man who is already dead, which demonstrates his expanding power. Furthermore, it foreshadows Luke 7:22, where Jesus tell John the Baptist's disciples, as proof of his ministry, that "the dead are raised up." The story of the raising of the widow's son in Nain is found only in Luke but has some similarities to the stories of Elijah raising the son of the widow of Zarephath (1 Kings 17:22-23) and of Elisha raising the son of the Shunemite woman (the town of Shunem was close to Nain; see 2 Kings 4:18-23). However, it is different in that Elijah and Elisha had to lay upon the boys and pray and breathe into them. Here Jesus raises this young man by a word of command.

> Soon afterward he went to a city called Nain, and his disciples and a great crowd went with him. As he drew near to the gate of the city, behold, a man who had died was being carried out, the only son of his mother, and she was a widow; and a large crowd from the city was with her. And when the Lord saw her, he had compassion on her and said to her, "Do not weep." (Luke 7:11-13)

The town of Nain is located on the very broad Jezreel Valley, just south of Mount Tabor and within eyeshot of Jesus' own hometown of Nazareth, on a hill northwest of Nain. The text mentions that Jesus "drew near to the gate of the city" (Luke 7:12), a scene similar to Elijah's approach to the Phoenician town of Zarephath: "So he [Elijah] arose and went to Zarephath; and when he came to the gate of the city, behold, a widow was there" (1 Kings 17:10).

The widow of Zarephath was preparing a last meal with her son before they starved to death when Elijah approached; the widow of Nain was already on her way to bury her only son. This situation is more dire even than that of Jairus, whose daughter was seriously ill but still alive when he approached Jesus (Mark 5:22). In Nain, Jesus is on his way into town, and he takes the initiative to speak to the widow; no one petitions him for anything.

Jesus is motivated to take this initiative because when he sees the widow grieving for her only son, "he had compassion on her" (Luke 7:13). Of all the funerals he might have witnessed, what motivated him to single out this particular widow with a special compassion as she wept in her grief? As mentioned, abo-his hometown of Nazareth was within eyeshot of this scene, where there lived another widow with an only son—a Son who knew he would die before she did, and in her presence. His compassion is especially stirred, knowing a son's pain at the thought of causing his beloved mother a sad grief. With tenderness he speaks to the widow gently: "Do not weep."

Our Lord demonstrates that loving our family and friends in this life on earth can stir up a compassion for other people, including people we have never met or known personally. We humans can draw upon our own past experiences, particularly the painful ones, and imagine the pain of others so vividly as to feel compassion for them. Authentic compassion requires us to move outside our experience of personal pain and love other people enough to sense their suffering and encounter them in their grief and sadness. Jesus knew the importance of compassion, and he changed course from his own mission for this widow.

Sadness, grief, and pain are inevitable in a world in which our loved ones get painfully sick, suffer, endure betrayals or disappointments, and eventually die. Some people seek to inoculate themselves against pain and grief by refusing to love other people or by "loving" them in a superficial way or in a way that uses them for their own selfish purposes. However, that only causes an even deeper pain of loneliness and radical isolation. Tragically, some individuals who have never experienced love as children are incapable of compassion or sincere love. Jesus was so loved—by his heavenly Father, by his earthly mother and foster father, and others—that he could enter deeply into compassion for even the strangers around him.

We might be tempted to think that God does not care for us in our pain and grief. He can seem too distant to really understand our problems, which we might consider too insignificant compared to the running of the vast universe. Yet here we see Jesus reaching out to a grief-stricken widow.

Think back on times when it seemed that God was too distant to care for your problems and pain. Then imagine that you are this widow in Nain. You may have heard rumors of a certain Jesus preaching around Galilee, but how could that be of interest to you—your husband and only child are dead. Yet now Jesus reaches out to you in loving compassion and tenderness. Spend time with Jesus considering your own deepest hurts, and let him comfort you. Seek to understand that his compassion is authentic, and accept it in your life.

Conclude with the prayer the Soul of Christ.

_____

_____

_____

_____

_____

_____

_____

_____

_____

_____

_____

_____

_____

_____

_____

_____

_____

_____

_____

_____

_____

_____

Jesus Raises the Young Man to Life

And he came and touched the bier, and the bearers stood still. And he said, "Young man, I say to you, arise." And the dead man sat up, and began to speak. And he gave him to his mother. Fear seized them all; and they glorified God, saying, "A great prophet has arisen among us!" and "God has visited his people!" And this report concerning him spread through the whole of Judea and all the surrounding country. (Luke 7:14-17)

The miracle begins with Jesus touching the bier of the dead man, even though the law taught that contact with a corpse made a person ritually unclean (see Numbers 19:11). As with the leper and the hemorrhaging woman, Jesus did not fear contact with people who could make him ritually unclean. Rather, just as he sought out sinners like the tax collector, he reached out to anyone in need of him. Amazingly, his touch of the unclean healed them, making them clean and incapable of spreading their impurity to him or anyone else.

The case of the dead young man is more amazing than that of the leper, who was considered the "walking dead." Here someone actually dead is told to rise and he does, speaking and being returned to his mother's embrace. Jesus' compassion for the bereft mother leads him to raise her son from the dead. This evokes fear, praise of God, and proclamations of faith in Jesus among the people, who exclaim, "A great prophet has arisen among us!" and "God has visited his people!" (Luke 7:16).

We would do well to consider each of these statements of faith in Jesus. Recall the Canticle of Zechariah, in which Zechariah opens the hymn by saying, "Blessed be the Lord God of Israel, / for he has visited and redeemed his people" (Luke 1:68). Zechariah means that this visitation refers to Mary's child, from "the house of his servant David" (1:69). The very phrase about "visiting" his people is now spoken by the people of Nain, who see Jesus' power to raise the dead.

Later Zechariah addresses his eight-day-old son, John, in this way: "And you, child, will be called the prophet of the Most High; / for you will go before the Lord to prepare his ways" (Luke 1:76). While Zechariah identifies his son, John, as the prophet who will prepare the way of the Lord, the witnesses to the raising of the young man say of Jesus that "a great prophet has arisen among us" (Luke 7:16). They are recognizing the fact that by Jesus' word, the young man was raised up, and therefore Jesus is acting like one of the prophets who spoke God's word and changed history. Immediately after this episode, some of John's disciples approach Jesus to ask if he is the one "who is to come" (7:19), which is a reference to the future prophet predicted in Malachi 3:1.

The reaction to this miracle raises another issue: who is this man that can accomplish such marvels? The apostles in the boat raised this question after Jesus had calmed the storm. The Pharisees raised it when he proclaimed the forgiveness of the paralytic's sins. The question will come up many other times as Jesus manifests ever-greater power and authority over sickness, disabilities, nature, and even death. It will culminate when Jesus himself raises the question that everyone else is thinking: "Who do men say that the Son of man is?" (Matthew 16:13; cf. Mark 8:27 and Luke 9:18). People will come up with a number of answers, as we see among the people of Nain.

Each of us today needs to better understand Jesus' identity and answer the questions raised by the witnesses of the raising of the young man, by the disciples of John the Baptist, and by Jesus himself: who do you say Jesus is? Do you believe in the miracles that the Gospel attributes to him, or were there natural explanations for them? Was Jesus just a prophet who did good deeds and taught about morality? These are the questions that come from both modern scholars and amateurs alike.

Imagine yourself standing before Jesus right after he raises the man from Nain. Speak to him about your own answers to the question "Who are you?" Engage him in a conversation about the reality of his miracles, their meaning, and their purpose. Then, with the people of Nain, glorify God with either the Gloria or the Glory Be.

_____

_____

_____

_____

_____

_____

_____

_____

_____

_____

_____

_____

_____

_____

CHAPTER 7

Storms at Sea

MATTHEW 8:18-27

Before the Journey, Two Men Want to Follow Jesus

Now when Jesus saw great crowds around him, he gave orders to go over to the other side. (Matthew 8:18)

Jesus had performed a number of healings and exorcisms, and the opposition to him from the Pharisees and Herodians had increased, even though (and probably because) the crowds kept growing in size and love of Jesus (see Mark 3). Though Jesus continued teaching the people (see 4:1-34), he decided to cross from the western side of the Sea of Galilee to the eastern side, where a predominantly Gentile population lived. The Romans had designated the region as the "Decapolis," meaning "ten cities," but the number of cities there was somewhat fluid. As Jesus ordered his disciples to sail the seven miles across the lake, two men spoke to Jesus about following him:

And a scribe came up and said to him, "Teacher, I will follow you wherever you go." And Jesus said to him, "Foxes have holes, and birds of the air have nests; but the Son of man has nowhere to lay his head." (Matthew 8:19-20)

The first man to speak up before Jesus departs to the other side is a scribe, that is, one of the scholars of the Pharisee party. Most of the time, the plural "scribes" describes Jesus' opponents or, on three occasions in Acts, the disciples' opponents. On three occasions in the Gospels, "scribe" is used in the singular, referring to an individual who is open to Jesus and his teaching (Matthew 8:19; 13:52; Mark 12:32).

This scribe addresses Jesus as "Teacher," a title by which rabbinic students addressed the man to whom they were devoted and from whom they wanted to learn. He enthusiastically offers to "follow" Jesus "wherever" he goes, but Jesus does not seek disciples who follow him on mere impulse, however enthusiastic they are.

In a section of teaching parables in Mark 4 that came immediately before this trip, Jesus relates the story of the seed that grew quickly among the rocks but died because it had no depth for its roots (Mark 4:5, 16-17). Jesus lays out for this scribe that Jesus, the "Son of Man" predicted in Daniel 7:13, has less shelter than the foxes or the birds. If the scribe is willing to accept this poverty with Jesus, then he can follow him. In fact, as the next two episodes make clear, following Jesus will even entail dangers, risks, and frightening events. St. Matthew did not record whether the scribe actually became one of Jesus' followers; wisely, he leaves that open-ended so that readers can consider the issue for themselves: am I willing to follow Jesus even if it entails poverty, insecurity, and danger?

> Another of the disciples said to him, "Lord, let me first go and bury my father." But Jesus said to him, "Follow me, and leave the dead to bury their own dead." (Matthew 8:21-22)

The second man is already one of Jesus' disciples. He, too, wants to join Jesus in the boat, but first he makes a very legitimate request: he wants to bury his father. "Honor your father and your mother" is one of the Ten Commandments (Exodus

20:12; Deuteronomy 5:16), and burial of the dead is an important act within Judaism:

> "My son, when I die, bury me, and do not neglect your mother." (Tobit 4:3)

> My son, let your tears fall for the dead, / and as one who is suffering grievously begin the lament. / Lay out his body with the honor due him, / and do not neglect his burial. / Let your weeping be bitter and your wailing fervent; / observe the mourning according to his merit. (Sirach 38:16-17)

And according to the *Mishna*, a book that comprises the oral traditions of the Jews, the religious obligations of reciting the daily Jewish prayers the *Shema* and *Tefilah* and of wearing phylacteries were less important even than burying the dead.

However, the Torah does mention one important exemption to the burial of dead parents, which involved the high priest:

> The priest who is chief among his brethren, upon whose head the anointing oil is poured, and who has been consecrated to wear the garments, shall not let the hair of his head hang loose, nor rend his clothes; he shall not go in to any dead body, nor defile himself, even for his father or for his mother. (Leviticus 21:10-11).

The prohibition of the high priest from burying even his father or mother is connected with that key element of the Israelite faith: God is the God of the living and not the dead. Contact with death makes a person ritually unclean, and the high priest must remain clean so as to perform his duties of offering sacrifice for the people of Israel.

In this light, Jesus' response, "Leave the dead to bury their own dead" (Matthew 8:22), is significant for two reasons. First, Jesus cannot delay his own journey across the sea in order to wait for this man to finish the process of burying his father. Jesus' mission has a greater urgency, and the mourning rites, which include sitting with mourners for a week after the burial, are a delay that his mission cannot afford.

Second, disciples need to understand that following Jesus is a priority as high as that of the ministry of the high priest. Jesus' response to the disciple would have been doubly shocking: he encouraged a disciple to follow him rather than bury a dead father, and he elevated the role of a disciple to that of the high priest. Jesus makes his entire mission, and therefore discipleship, an urgent matter, since it is the kingdom of God, and it is the needs of the people living in darkness that are at stake.

Imagine yourself as the disciple whose father has just died. How would you feel if Jesus said to you, "Leave the dead to bury their own dead"? Would you have understood the urgency of Jesus' mission? Would you have been tempted to get on the boat with Jesus, or would you have wanted to stay at home to bury your father? To what might Jesus be calling you now that would require you to abandon something dear to you? Talk to Jesus about it. What does he say to you? What do you say to him?

Conclude with an Our Father.

_____

_____

_____

The Journey across the Sea of Galilee

And when he got into the boat, his disciples followed him. (Matthew 8:23)

The disciples follow Jesus into the boat and carry out his orders to cross the Sea of Galilee. This would have been quite normal for them, since at least four of them were fishermen who made their living on the Sea of Galilee. However, following Jesus does not always mean that everything will go smoothly, easily, or with the success that humans define. In this case, following Jesus will lead to a highly dangerous, risky situation.

And behold, there arose a great storm on the sea, so that the boat was being swamped by the waves; but he was asleep. (Matthew 8:24)

Once while I was sailing across the Sea of Galilee with a large group of pilgrims, a woman asked me how it could be that dangerous storms could rise up on the Sea of Galilee, which is only twelve miles by seven miles. Rather than tell her myself, I went to one of the sailors on our boat and asked him about it. Not only did his voice assure us of the power of the storms on the lake where he worked every day, but the wideness of his eyes also affirmed it. One reason is that the dominant northwesterly winds pass through the narrow Valley of the Doves, just west of the sea, focusing the force of the wind directly on the water. The storm described here endangered the boat and all the men in it. Meanwhile, Jesus sleeps calmly through it all; not even the water washing over the gunwales wakes him from his deep sleep.

> And they went and woke him, saying, "Save, Lord; we are perishing." And he said to them, "Why are you afraid, O men of little faith?" (Matthew 8:25-26a)

Overwhelmed by the danger, the disciples in the boat wake Jesus, probably quite amazed that he could sleep through such a storm. Their words to him are an order: "Save, Lord." Recall that during Joseph's dream, the angel told him to name the son that his betrothed, Mary, was going to bear "Jesus" because "he will save his people from their sins" (Matthew 1:21). Here, there is a play on the meaning of his name when the disciples ask him to save them because "we are perishing" (8:25).

Just as astounding as Jesus' ability to sleep through a violent storm is his question: "Why are you afraid, O men of little faith?" The obvious reason they are afraid is that their boat is sinking in the great storm. However, Jesus' question about their fear is inherently connected to his description of them as "men of little faith." On the Sermon on the Mount, he had addressed the people as "men of little faith" (Matthew 6:30) as he taught that God the Father knows their needs and would provide for them more surely than he would feed the birds of the air or clothe the lilies of the field. Jesus then concluded,

> "But seek first his kingdom and his righteousness, and all these things shall be yours as well. Therefore do not be anxious about tomorrow, for tomorrow will be anxious for itself. Let the day's own trouble be sufficient for the day." (6:33-34)

The disciples need to focus on seeking the kingdom of God and his righteousness and have confidence in God's plan to provide for their "daily bread" and other needs. That is the basis for faith that eliminates anxiety.

This kind of faith was at stake in Jesus' words to the scribe that wanted to follow him: the Son of Man has less shelter than the foxes and birds; do you have enough faith to trust in God as completely as Jesus, who leads these adventures? This teaching on faith is the backdrop for Jesus' question to the disciples about their fear. He knew that the real issue was their lack of faith.

The world remains a difficult and frightening place. The very forces that bring life can also bring death: rain for the crops can become a flood; winds can become hurricanes or tornadoes; fire that cooks and warms can burn down whole forests. Yet Christ wants us to live amid the many risks of life with a type of faith that trusts in our Father's providence, even when we are tempted to be frightened. When she could not perceive his presence in difficult trials, St. Thérèse of Lisieux said, "I knew that Jesus was there, asleep in my boat."

Consider some of the dangers and difficulties you have experienced in life, especially those times when it seemed that Jesus was asleep in the boat. How did you handle those situations? What happened as a result of the circumstance? Speak now to Jesus about it. Picture him waking up from a deep sleep on a boat in stormy seas. What would you say to him about your troubles? What might he say back to you? Speak to him as a friend to a friend, conversing about your concerns and listening to him.

Conclude with the prayer the Soul of Christ.

_____

_____

_____

_____

_____

_____

_____

_____

_____

_____

_____

_____

_____

_____

_____

_____

_____

_____

_____

_____

Jesus Rebukes the Sea

Then he rose and rebuked the winds and the sea; and there was a great calm. (Matthew 8:26b)

Having been awakened, Jesus gives proof for placing faith in him by calming the wind and the sea through his word. Jesus' command is described as a "rebuke" to the wind and the waves. The Old Testament portrayal of the Lord's relationship with the sea gives some insight into this passage. When the Lord addresses Job after his long complaints, he asks Job a series of rhetorical questions, including one about the Lord's relationship to the sea:

Or who shut in the sea with doors, / when it burst forth from the womb; / when I made clouds its garment, / and thick darkness its swaddling band, / and prescribed bounds for it, / and set bars and doors, / and said, "Thus far shall you come, and no farther, / and here shall your proud waves be stayed"? (Job 38:8-11)

The implied answer is that the Lord gave orders to the sea and "stayed" its proud waves, while Job, a mere man, could not demonstrate such power.

A number of psalms describe the Lord God as having power over the sea, using some ancient Canaanite ideas of the sea as an enemy that slaps at the shoreline with its waves, like a force trying to devour the dry land. Yet in Israel's psalms, God is in complete control of the sea:

By dread deeds you answer us with deliverance, / O God of our salvation, / who are the hope of all the ends of the earth, / and of the farthest seas; / who by your strength have established the mountains, / being girded with might; / who still the roaring of the seas, / the roaring of their waves, / the tumult of the peoples. (Psalm 65:5-7)

The "God of our salvation" has the power to still "the roaring of the seas, the roaring of their waves." Here are other psalms that allude to this idea:

You rule the raging of the sea; / when its waves rise, you still them. (Psalm 89:9)

The floods have lifted up, O LORD, / the floods have lifted up their voice, / the floods lift up their roaring. / Mightier than the thunders of many waters, / mightier than the waves of the sea, the LORD on high is mighty! (Psalm 93:3-4)

You covered it with the deep as with a garment; / the waters stood above the mountains. / At your rebuke they fled; / at the sound of your thunder they took to flight. (Psalm 104:6-7)

Then they cried to the LORD in their trouble, / and he delivered them from their distress; / he made the storm be still, / and the waves of the sea were hushed. (Psalm 107:28-29)

These many texts all indicate that the One who has control of the sea, who orders it to find its limits or to be still, is the Lord God himself.

In this Gospel passage, Jesus makes the same kind of command as the Lord God in the Old Testament passages, and his command is fulfilled exactly as and when he speaks it. Just as we saw Jesus' divinity, when by his word he forgave the sins of the paralytic and then commanded him to get up and walk, so too do we see Jesus' divinity shown in his calming of the sea.

Throughout Christian history, theologians, and many believers as well, have swung from either overemphasizing Jesus' humanity or his divinity. The temptation is to focus on one of his natures to the neglect and, in the case of many different kinds of heresies, even the denial of one nature over the other. Arius denied Jesus' divinity; various Monophysites denied his humanity. In this passage we consider that the truly human Jesus was brought across the sea in a boat and fell very soundly asleep—sleep being the one activity humans do more than any other. Yet Jesus controlled the same sea by a word that had divine authority.

Consider the ways in which you think about Jesus' humanity and divinity. Do you so focus on his humanity as to dismiss his miracles, his divine dignity, and his worthiness to be worshipped? Is he so much a friend that adoration of Jesus is far from your mind? Or do you so focus on his divinity that he seems completely remote from human experience, unable to understand what you go through? Speak to Jesus about this tension as you personally experience it. What might he say to you about it?

Conclude with the prayers the Soul of Christ and the Glory Be.

_____

_____

_____

_____

_____

_____

_____

_____

_____

_____

_____

_____

_____

_____

_____

_____

_____

_____

_____

_____

The Disciples Marvel at Jesus

And the men marveled, saying, "What sort of man is this, that even winds and sea obey him?" (Matthew 8:27)

Having been steeped in the Old Testament, especially in the psalms, a key component of Jewish prayer, the disciples ask the obvious question: "What sort of man is this?" They connect the question with his power to cause the winds and waves to obey him, just as the Lord God does in the Old Testament. However, these "men of little faith" (Matthew 8:26) are not yet capable of putting all the pieces together; they do not yet see the whole picture because they do not yet know how to connect the dots.

Like them, we are gradually learning that the process of following Jesus into various adventures becomes the one way to learn about the things he can do. By living the adventures of life with Jesus close to us, we, too, gain clues about his true identity. Few people come to understand Jesus through abstract reasoning; most come to know him in the concrete circumstances of his life and ministry. They come to see that something much more than a man is revealed through all of his actions, even though he shows himself as truly a man who sleeps, eats, hungers, and weeps—all that comprises the human experience. Yet Jesus always remains someone far beyond human capabilities and expectations.

The disciples simply "marveled" at him. They were filled with wonder that the man they needed to shake from deep slumber could calm the seas. We also learn from them the importance of wonder. Jesus presents a series of mysteries whose comprehension is beyond our ordinary categories of life. The apostles will be filled with amazement at every step of the way as they follow Jesus. Even when they see him raised from the dead, they will try to place him in their own more familiar even if frightening category of seeing a ghost. However, only by staying faithful to Jesus and to all that he does will the disciples discover the truth about him. They will even touch the "ghost" and watch him eat so that he can take them to a new category: the resurrection of the dead (see Luke 24:37-43).

Later, after his ascension into heaven, Jesus will send these same disciples on further adventures. These same "men of little faith" will be hauled into the Sanhedrin and defend their preaching about Jesus with boldness: "There is salvation in no one else, for there is no other name under heaven given among men by which we must be saved" (Acts 4:12). They who with their little faith cried out, "Lord, save us!" eventually come to learn that truly no one besides Jesus can save them.

Consider your faith at this point in your life. Are you filled with great faith, or do you sometimes experience doubts? Imagine being with Jesus in the boat on the smooth surface of the Sea of Galilee. Having gone through the dangerous waves but now sailing to shore in calm and safety, speak to him about your willingness to follow him through yet more adventures. Speak of your own amazement at having survived the storms of your own life. Was your faith intact? Did your faith grow? Did it get challenged to near nonexistence? What might he say to you about your present state of faith? Speak to him and listen carefully to all that he might say to you.

Conclude with the prayer the Soul of Christ.

_____

_____

_____

_____

_____

_____

_____

_____

_____

_____

_____

_____

_____

_____

_____

_____

_____

_____

_____

_____

_____

CHAPTER 8

The Healing of the Hemorrhaging Woman and Jairus' Daughter

MARK 5:21-43

The Background to the Miracles

And when Jesus had crossed again in the boat to the other side, a great crowd gathered about him; and he was beside the sea. (Mark 5:21)

Jesus has crossed back from the eastern Gentile side to the western Jewish side of the Sea of Galilee, where issues related to Judaism will come to the fore. Mark will show Jesus crossing back and forth across the Sea of Galilee a number of times, performing miracles on the Gentile side of the lake that parallel the miracles he performed on the Jewish side. (The first miracle on the Jewish side was an exorcism in the synagogue in Capernaum, and the first miracle on the Gentile side was an exorcism of the demoniac with the legion of demons [Mark 1:21-28; 5:1-20].) This shows that Christ's mission is first to Israel but also includes the Gentiles.

Then came one of the rulers of the synagogue, Jairus by name; and seeing him, he fell at his feet, and besought him, saying, "My little daughter is at the point of death. Come and lay your hands on her, so that she may be made well, and live." (Mark 5:22-23)

The synagogue was a Pharisaic institution established to teach people the Scriptures on the Sabbath, so Jairus, the head of the synagogue, belonged to that party. The Hebrew form of his name, "Jair," appears seven times in the Old Testament, meaning "He will give light," and twice from a different Hebrew root meaning "He will raise." Perhaps Mark included his name because members of his community knew Jairus, but Matthew does not name him.

Earlier, in Mark 2–3, Jesus' growing authority gave rise to a number of disputes with the Pharisees. We have no way of knowing whether Jairus was involved at all in these disputes with Jesus; we can only guess. However, now that Jairus' daughter is dying, these disagreements have faded in importance. Jairus' love for his daughter now evokes faith, as with the woman who washed Jesus' feet and was forgiven because she loved much; this was counted as a faith that saved her (Luke 7:48-50). Jairus seeks out Jesus' power to heal, specifically asking him to "lay your hands on her" as a recognition that power flows from physical contact with Jesus.

For his part, Jesus does not stop and demand that Jairus cease taking part in or supporting the Pharisees' disputes with him but goes with him to his house. We can learn from our blessed Lord's example in regard to people who may have offended us or who oppose us. When we see signs of love and faith, we can learn from Jesus, who fanned those signs from a smoldering wick into flame:

He will not wrangle or cry aloud, / nor will any one hear his voice in the streets; / he will not break a bruised reed / or quench a smoldering wick, / till he brings justice to victory; / and in his name will the Gentiles hope. (Matthew 12:19-21)

How do you encourage the glimmers of faith and love in someone who is distant from the Church or even opposes and hates it? How do you look for a spark in the smoldering wicks of faith in people whose lives are not right or whose ideology is opposed to Christianity? Ask Jesus for the grace to cherish the goal of fanning the tiniest sparks of faith, hope, and love into great flames that light the world. What might he say to you about the ways you can approach people whose faith has faded? Is there one person he puts on your heart whom you can approach? How might he help you?

Conclude with the prayer the Soul of Christ.

_____

_____

_____

_____

_____

_____

_____

_____

_____

_____

_____

_____

_____

_____

_____

MEDITATION 2

The Hemorrhaging Woman Seeks a Healing

And he went with him. And a great crowd followed him and thronged about him. And there was a woman who had had a flow of blood for twelve years, and who had suffered much under many physicians, and had spent all that she had, and was no better but rather grew worse. She had heard the reports about Jesus, and came up behind him in the crowd and touched his garment. (Mark 5:24-27)

As they go to Jairus' house, attention shifts from the urgency of the little girl's sickness to the large crowd and one particular woman. She is unnamed, but there is a lengthy description of her current condition: her twelve-year flow of blood has caused her to spend all of her money on doctors who have only made her worse. By the way, St. Luke, who is identified as a physician (Colossians 4:14), simply says that she "could not be healed by any one" (Luke 8:43), which is perhaps a professional courtesy to other doctors who had tried but failed to heal her. This flow of blood made the woman ritually unclean and therefore unable to join the community in worship. (Blood was sacred, the seat of life in Judaism, so any flow of blood precluded a person from entering the Temple.)

Placing the story of the hemorrhaging woman within that of Jairus' daughter is a technique by which the two episodes interpret one another. Notice that the older woman's hemorrhage began when Jairus' daughter was born, twelve years earlier, though neither event was otherwise linked to the other.

> For she said, "If I touch even his garments, I shall be made well." And immediately the hemorrhage ceased; and she felt in her body that she was healed of her disease. (Mark 5:28-29)

The focus here is on the woman's faith. She believed that she could be healed by merely touching Jesus' garments (an act that would make him ritually unclean because of her hemorrhage). While medicine had failed her, touching Jesus brought her healing, and she could feel it in her body.

This woman had been hemorrhaging for at least ten or more years before Jesus began his public ministry. Earlier, when crowds of people were approaching Jesus for exorcisms and healing during his stays in Capernaum, she did not approach him. Was she reticent because her constant bleeding made her unclean? We can only speculate. Yet even here she approaches Jesus surreptitiously, not making a public request, not making a show of her disorder or her search for a healing. She considers the tactic of touching the hem of his garment all within her own mind, without saying anything to anyone else. Yet this is still counted as enough faith to receive God's healing.

How strongly do you believe that Christ can actually improve your life? Are you afraid to speak your faith out loud because of what others might think of you? Do you want to keep your act of faith personal, private, and hidden? If so, why? Speak to Jesus about the attitude you have toward your faith. What might he say to you in that regard? What does he want you to do about making your faith in him known?

Conclude with the prayer the Soul of Christ.

_____

_____

_____

_____

_____

_____

_____

_____

_____

_____

_____

_____

_____

_____

_____

_____

_____

_____

_____

_____

Jesus Reacts to Power Going Out from Him

And Jesus, perceiving in himself that power had gone forth from him, immediately turned about in the crowd, and said, "Who touched my garments?" And his disciples said to him, "You see the crowd pressing around you, and yet you say, 'Who touched me?'" And he looked around to see who had done it. (Mark 5:30-32)

When the woman senses the healing, Jesus feels power go forth from him. His question "Who touched me?" seems absurd to the disciples, who could merely observe the crowd pushing and pressing on him. However, Jesus continues to look for the individual who has touched him in a manner different from the crowd.

But the woman, knowing what had been done to her, came in fear and trembling and fell down before him, and told him the whole truth. And he said to her, "Daughter, your faith has made you well; go in peace, and be healed of your disease." (Mark 5:33-34)

The woman, who has been bold enough to "steal" a quick touch of Jesus' garment in order to be healed, now feels "fear and trembling" in the face of being caught. She apparently fears that she may have taken some power from him or diminished him by seeking his healing power. However, Jesus does not look for her to accuse her of any wrongdoing, nor does he want to rebuke her for receiving a healing without explicit permission from him. Rather, he wants to address her as "Daughter" to show that he sees her touch as the start of a filial relationship with her. Then he explains to her that her faith has healed her, so she can go in peace. Rather than rebuking her, he wants to speak to her and take a more active role in her healing. Receiving his power and healing is not the primary issue in having faith; rather, it is the relationship with Jesus that matters most, and Jesus wants to establish that relationship very clearly and explicitly.

Because of her faith, the woman is distinguished from the crowd that is touching Jesus. Their touch shows their attraction to Jesus' celebrity; her touch shows confident faith.

As Catholics, we can reflect on the way we approach the Holy Eucharist and the other sacraments. Do we stand in line with a crowd "pressing around" Jesus, or do we receive him in the Eucharist with an expectant faith in his power to heal us, as we state in the prayer before reception, "Lord, I am not worthy that you should enter under my roof, but only say the word and my soul shall be healed." That quote of the centurion (cf. Matthew 8:8) professes not only humility but also expectant faith that Jesus' presence within us will make a difference in our lives. If the hemorrhaging woman could muster expectant faith from touching Jesus' garments, how much more should we expect by receiving his Body, Blood, Soul, and Divinity in Holy Communion.

The Lord does not want a hidden faith that seeks his power outside a relationship of love. Nor does he want us to be like those in the crowd, bumping into him in an impersonal way. He truly loves us and wants to engage us ever more personally. What might you do to engage our Lord more personally when you receive Holy Communion? What change in attitude may be necessary in you to avoid any rote reception of him in the Eucharist? How can you deepen your experience of touching him with the faith of the woman? What can you do to enter a more intimate relationship with Jesus that allows you to be called "Son" or "Daughter"? Imagine being someone in the crowd, and speak to Jesus about what he wants from you. What might he say?

Conclude with the prayers the Soul of Christ and the Our Father.

_____

_____

_____

_____

_____

_____

_____

_____

_____

_____

_____

_____

_____

_____

_____

_____

The Healing of Jairus' Daughter

While he was still speaking, there came from the ruler's house some who said, "Your daughter is dead. Why trouble the Teacher any further?" But ignoring what they said, Jesus said to the ruler of the synagogue, "Do not fear, only believe." (Mark 5:35-36)

During this short delay on the way to Jairus' house, the daughter has died, and messengers bring that news. Note how these messengers assume that Jesus is being "troubled" by Jairus' request. Addressing Jesus simply as "the Teacher," they understand Jesus only on a human level, so they reduce him to the level of simply another teacher whose ideas may be respectable but are simply human teaching with no apparent power. Further, because they consider him merely human, they also assume that he would be uninterested in being "troubled" by running after various petitions and requests.

For his part, Jesus "ignores" their perceptions of him and apparently does not consider Jairus' request a bother at all. Rather, as with the hemorrhaging woman, he urges Jairus to forego fear and "only believe." Jesus centers on the mystery of faith as a decision by human beings. Certainly faith is a gift from God, a grace that makes it possible to enter a proper relationship with him. Yet here as elsewhere, Jesus tells people to believe because they have a role to play by embracing the gift of faith. Humans are not passive recipients of faith, because there must be a mutual relationship between God and individual persons. God takes the initiative in the relationship, as is the case here where Jesus encourages Jairus' faith. However, he also recognizes Jairus' side of the equation by instructing him not to fear but only to believe. This is true particularly in situations in which the natural means have come to a complete end—the little girl is dead. At this point, only God can act, so Jesus summons faith from Jairus.

Too often we are like the messengers who speak and act as if Jesus were just a human being onto whom we can project our own small-minded ideas of God. We can be tempted to think of God in our own image and miss the mystery of his infinite majesty and greatness. We too easily forget that he is beyond us and will act more powerfully than we can even begin to imagine.

Imagine yourself as Jairus at the moment the messengers arrive with the news that your beloved daughter is dead. You are faced with a choice to believe two conflicting messages: do not trouble the teacher further, or fear not, only believe. Our human nature is naturally inclined to the first message. What do you think when the words of your daughter's death reach your ears? What do you think when Jesus gives you his message against fear and for faith? Speak to Jesus about these messages. What might he say to you about the way in which you have acted in similar crises of faith in the past? What have been the comparable crises in your own life? How did you react? Speak to Jesus about that.

Conclude with the prayer the Soul of Christ.

_____

_____

_____

Inside Jairus' House

And he allowed no one to follow him except Peter and James and John the brother of James. When they came to the house of the ruler of the synagogue, he saw a tumult, and people weeping and wailing loudly. And when he had entered, he said to them, "Why do you make a tumult and weep? The child is not dead but sleeping." And they laughed at him. But he put them all outside, and took the child's father and mother and those who were with him, and went in where the child was. (Mark 5:37-40)

This is the first of at least three occasions when an inner circle of three disciples is chosen from among the inner circle of twelve disciples. (The Transfiguration and the agony in Gethsemane are the other two occasions when Peter, James, and John are the only disciples present.) Why these three? Later, Peter will be the leader of all disciples, James will be the first apostle to die, and John will be the last apostle to die. Each of them has a distinctive role as a witness to Jesus, and at this point he has chosen them to witness to his power over death.

Upon entering the house, many people are weeping and lamenting, which is characteristic of the typically unrestrained expression of grief in Middle Eastern society. Jesus addresses the tumult of mourners and asserts that the little girl is only asleep—a common idiom for death, but not on this occasion. The laments turn to laughter, making his question yet more insightful: "Why do you make a tumult and weep?" (Mark 5:39). The quick change of emotion indicates a certain insincerity among the mourners, so he orders the mourners out of the house when they make his statement of faith the object of their ridicule. The mourners are hindrances to faith, and he permits only five believers—the parents and the three disciples—to enter the room.

Jesus did not consider mourning and grief evils in themselves, since he had proclaimed in the Beatitudes, "Blessed are those who mourn, for they shall be comforted" (Matthew 5:4). The problem in Jairus' home was the apparent insincerity of these mourners, who resorted to cynical ridicule when Jesus informed them that the girl was simply sleeping. They did not have faith in Jesus or his word, and the blessedness of mourning did not apply to them. They simply expressed emotions, perhaps as professional mourners who were often paid for their skill in evoking emotion among the people who sincerely mourned the lost loved one. Such professionals did not actually love the people present; they provided a service of emotional release. Jesus refused to tolerate their insincerity, lack of love, or lack of faith, and he sent them outside, judging them unworthy to be present at the raising of the little girl.

Authentic mourning and grief at the death of a loved one can be an implicit act of natural faith, indicating an innate intuition that life is supposed to go on forever. Theoretically, people know that death is inevitable, but the actual experience of losing someone brings grief. Why? Perhaps because humans know that life is meant for eternity, but that does not happen during our time on earth. Such implicit faith can become the natural basis upon which God's grace of hope can build, and that may be one reason it is blessed to mourn.

Our Lord can certainly deal with sincere human emotion, including grief, since it implies a certain natural faith and a sincere love for the dead. What he does not tolerate is playacting that covers up a lack of love, faith, and hope. The Greek work "hypocrite" actually means a "play actor," someone who takes on a role other than his own. Such were the mourners who could turn their wailing and lamenting into laughter on a dime.

The parents could feel the empty place in their hearts as they saw their daughter lying dead; they were missing her already. Yet they let Jesus into the room, which indicated that they still had faith in him. Like Jairus and his wife, we can present Jesus with our deepest difficulties and griefs, maintaining the truth of our feelings but also approaching him with loving faith. He desires to be present with us in those moments, and he wants us to invite him to share them with him.

Examine your own life to see if there have been times when you have been inauthentic with God, like the mourners. Think about times when you have tried to present the way you were supposed to feel, but you actually hid or denied your authentic feelings, ideas, or attitudes. Those are moments when God often seems absent.

Then consider those times you have authentically presented your true fears, your actual sins, and the motives behind them before Christ in complete honesty. Have not those been the times of deepest intimacy with him? Does he not come closer to you the more open and honest you are? Speak to him about these widely different moments of your spiritual life, and conclude with the prayer the Soul of Christ.

_____

_____

_____

_____

Jesus Raises the Little Girl

Taking her by the hand he said to her, "Talitha cumi"; which means, "Little girl, I say to you, arise." And immediately the girl got up and walked; for was twelve years old. And they were immediately they were overcome with amazement. And he strictly charged them that no one should know this, and told them to give her something to eat. (Mark 5:41-43)

As St. Mark does in other verses, he includes Jesus' original words in Aramaic, with a translation afterward (see Mark 3:17; 7:11, 34; 11:9-10; 14:36; 15:22, 34). This technique of using the original language was popular in ancient Rome, and some modern people still use it, as when they include Hebrew words in modern hymns.

Much more important is that Jesus' human touch and his authoritative word work together again to effect a miracle. Just as touching the leper (Mark 1:41) or the hemorrhaging woman (5:28-30) would make Jesus ritually unclean, so also would touching the little girl's corpse. However, his command to the little girl to arise "immediately" causes her to get up and walk; she is no longer dead. As in the previous two cases, Jesus does not contract the contagion of uncleanness from the people around him; instead, they receive a transformation that heals them.

Jesus exercises authority once again, as he did with his teaching (Mark 1:22), with the demons (1:26-28), with his other miracles, and even over the sabbath regulations (2:23–3:6). However, here he has authority over death and life, raising a dead girl by his touch and words. As a result, the five witnesses—the inner circle of three apostles and the two parents—were "immediately . . . overcome with amazement" (Mark 5:42).

Within this passage, an older woman with a twelve-year hemorrhage was healed and made "clean" by Jesus, whose touch stopped the flow of blood that separated her from the worshipping community; then, a twelve-year-old newly dead girl was raised by the touch of Jesus' hand and the authority of his word. Central to both episodes is the necessity of faith in Jesus. Whether one believes before he speaks (as with the woman) or whether one accepts his summons to believe (as with Jairus), Jesus acts powerfully for those in a faith relationship with him.

Further, when there is faith, Jesus then draws the believer into a deeper relationship with him. He speaks to the woman, who wanted her faith to remain anonymous and unnoticed, so that he can announce that salvation belongs to her because she believed. He draws three disciples and the two parents into the room privately to raise up the little girl and then tells them to keep this miracle to themselves. This latter statement shows that he does not seek fame for miracle working but rather desires the intimacy of their faith in him.

Jesus is also inviting us to ever-deeper levels of faith. It will not be miracles but the personal relationship that raises us to eternal life. The healed woman and the resuscitated little girl eventually died; faith in Jesus that leads one to an ever-deepening relationship with him lasts for eternity, and such is the gift of salvation he offers to everyone who believes his gospel.

Take time to wonder at Jesus and the life of faith to which he has called you. Give him thanks for this gift and ask him to deepen it, especially at times of great crisis, such as when you or your loved ones are very sick, or your loved ones have died.

Invite Jesus into the inner room of your life where your most personal hurts, suffering, and pain exist, and ask him to bring you healing and transformation. But also offer him your whole and most sincere self. Give him the full truth of your experiences and personality. He can deal with anything you give him except phony and false self-images. Give the truth of yourself to him so that he who is the truth (John 14:6) can meet you at your deepest core and accept you with the fullness of his divine, infinite love.

Conclude with the Glory Be or the Gloria from the Mass.

_____

_____

_____

_____

_____

_____

_____

_____

_____

_____

_____

_____

_____

_____

CHAPTER 9

The Multiplication of the Loaves and Fish

MATTHEW 14:12-22

Jesus and the Disciples Sail to a Lonely Place

And his disciples came and took the body and buried it; and they went and told Jesus. Now when Jesus heard this, he withdrew from there in a boat to a lonely place apart. But when the crowds heard it, they followed him on foot from the towns. As he went ashore he saw a great throng; and he had compassion on them, and healed their sick. (Matthew 14:12-14)

St. Matthew begins this scene with John's disciples telling Jesus about the Baptist's death and burial. Just as John's arrest had been a signal for Jesus to begin his public ministry in Galilee (Matthew 4:12-17), now John's execution is a signal for Jesus to set out for a lonely place, apart from the crowds. This ought to be compared to Jesus' withdrawal from the crowds in Capernaum when "he prayed" and discerned that the next stage of his ministry was to go out to the other towns in Galilee (Mark 1:35, 38). So here he goes out alone to pray and presumably discern the next stage of his ministry.

However, the crowds follow Jesus, watching him sail along and disembark at the "lonely place" away from the towns. This site is now known by its Arabic name, Tabgha, based on a mispronunciation of the Greek word for "Seven Springs," a name that comes from John's description of the place as well watered with an abundance of grass (6:10; Matthew 14:19). Nearby are the remnants of a first-century breakwater where boats could be safely moored.

Though the crowd thwarts Jesus' plan to be alone, his love and compassion for these needy folk overwhelm his plan for solitude, and he heals their sick. Many of the sick had been unable to follow his journey without help from other people leading or carrying them. On that assumption, it is easy to see that Jesus' overwhelming and powerfully effective compassion is a response to the care and compassion of the many people caring for the sick and needy. They do what they are able to accomplish—they bring him their sick. Jesus does what he alone can accomplish—he heals the people by his divine power.

This is not the first time that Jesus' plan changes based on a request for a miracle. At Cana his Mother informed him of the host's lack of wine, and he raised the issue that it was not yet his hour (John 2:1-11). His compassion at that moment led to one miracle, and his compassion here in this deserted place leads him to perform many miracles. In both situations, people simply and lovingly seek him, and Jesus responds even though it is not in accord with his prepared plan. The simple love of humans evokes his love in action.

We would do well to consider that our weaknesses, our sincere searching for him, and our humble love are what evoke Jesus' compassion and mutual love, not requests that can seem like demands because they are tainted with an attitude of entitlement. Jesus cherishes our confidence in him, especially when we seek him with focused attention.

Place yourself in the crowd that followed the progress of his boat by walking along the shoreline to the place where it landed. What are you seeking from him? What is the most important concern you would want to lay before Jesus from your life today? Picture yourself doing that in a lonely place on the shore of the Sea of Galilee. As Jesus shows compassion toward you, what does his face look like? What might there be in Jesus that would evoke your confidence in presenting him with your need? Speak to him about both your need and his compassionate response to you.

Conclude with the prayer the Soul of Christ.

_____

_____

_____

_____

_____

_____

_____

_____

_____

_____

_____

_____

_____

_____

_____

_____

_____

_____

MEDITATION 2

The Disciples Present Jesus with a Problem

When it was evening, the disciples came to him and said, "This is a lonely place, and the day is now over; send the crowds away to go into the villages and buy food for themselves." Jesus said, "They need not go away; you give them something to eat." They said to him, "We have only five loaves here and two fish." And he said, "Bring them here to me." (Matthew 14:15-18)

Jesus' disciples now point out a new problem: the crowds cannot get food in the "lonely place," so they need to be dismissed to buy some in the nearby villages. Their request manifests both compassion for the people and anxiety about the problem. Others who perceived problems brought them to Jesus: for example, Jesus' mother saw the lack of wine at Cana (John 2:1-11); the leper told of his need for cleansing (Mark 1:40-45); and Martha asked for help from Mary (Luke 10:38-42). Unlike Jesus' mother, however, who instructed the servants in Cana to do whatever Jesus told them (John 2:5), here the disciples give Jesus their own solution to the problem: send the people away to buy food for themselves. They see only the lack of food, and they offer a human solution based on self-sufficiency.

Jesus then offers a suggestion: "You give them something to eat" (Matthew 14:16). Again, the disciples see only what they lack—five loaves and two fish would not satisfy the disciples and Jesus, yet alone the crowd. However, Jesus sees beyond the lack to a possibility that far exceeds the disciples' imagination to deal with this enormous problem. He tells them to bring the resources they already have, the five loaves and two fish. (Presumably, the fish, available on the west side of the Sea of Galilee, are those known today as St. Peter's fish, a large, delicious subtropical bass that is still commonly eaten.) The disciples have no idea what he will do, but he is clearly in charge of this situation in a way that perplexes them.

Consider times in the past when you were faced with problems, particularly ones that were both overwhelming and unavoidable. My mother, Lorraine, on the last Christmas before she died, told us children, "I have absolutely no idea how we fed, clothed, and housed you children, because we never had the money to do so, but somehow we always had enough. God did that for us." While raising the four of us, Mom and Dad were full of anxiety, which was visible to us children, even though we did not understand its causes until we grew up. Yet only in retrospect could my mom and dad see that despite their many worries, God had helped them with their needs as they were raising their family.

Many other families can relate their own experiences of having been out in a lonely place with only God to help. Many individuals who have gone through difficult times, such as being seriously ill or surviving a war or natural disaster, recognize in retrospect that they had only the equivalent of five loaves and two fish but somehow managed.

Consider your own experiences when you had very little to work with. Picture yourself being like the apostles who handed that little bit to Jesus when he asked for it. Speak to Jesus about your past or present anxieties over difficult situations. What does he say to you about your focus on how little you have? What might he ask you to do with that little bit that is overwhelmed by your needs?

Conclude with an Our Father.

_____

_____

_____

_____

_____

_____

_____

_____

_____

_____

_____

_____

_____

_____

_____

_____

_____

_____

_____

_____

_____

_____

Jesus Multiplies the Loaves and Fish

Then he ordered the crowds to sit down on the grass; and taking the five loaves and the two fish he looked up to heaven, and blessed, and broke and gave the loaves to the disciples, and the disciples gave them to the crowds. (Matthew 14:19)

First, Jesus orders the crowds to sit on the abundant grass in this well-watered area, an action that lets the thousands of people there present know that another stage of Jesus' activity is about to begin.

Second, he takes the five loaves and two fish and looks to heaven, the source of all God's blessings, to pray as all Jews do before they eat bread: "Blessed are you, Lord God of the universe, who brings forth bread from the earth." As Jesus gazes toward heaven for the blessing, he is doing more than drawing ordinary bread from the earth, as stated in the Jewish blessing. As he hinted in John 6, this was an event closer to Israel's receiving manna, the bread from heaven in the wilderness.

Third, Jesus breaks the bread—a practice that is still normal among the people of the Holy Land, whether Jew, Christian, or Muslim. For their meals, each person breaks a piece of bread from a round loaf and eats a bit of food with each broken fragment.

Finally, Jesus gives the loaves to the disciples and they give the loaves to the crowd. In doing this, Jesus lets the disciples share in the action of which they are capable after he has performed the miracle, which only he, God-made-man, can accomplish.

Some interpretations of this story claim that the real miracle was Jesus inducing the people to share the food they had hidden under their garments, which some preachers still try to assert. However, that has nothing in common with the Gospels. Jesus' actions and words did not mention having the crowd share the food; St. John mentions a little boy with "five barley loaves and two fish" (6:9), but no one else has any food. Such rationalizations make nonsense out of the Evangelists' reports of the miracle as well as the crowd's reaction. All four Evangelists describe this miracle as an action of God; Jesus' miracle exceeded even that which the Father had done in the wilderness.

Picture yourself among the people seated on the grass in large groups. What would you be thinking as you sat there and watched Jesus look up to heaven and give thanks for the five loaves and two fish? Would you join him in that act of gratitude and prayer? If so, what would you be thinking during that pause in his miracle working as you realize your own stomach is empty?

Then consider your reaction as you witness the twelve disciples handing out bread and fish to everyone. What would cross your mind as you realize that you, along with the whole large crowd, would have your fill of bread and fish? Consider your reaction to eating with everyone else: what would your feelings be? Finally, picture yourself going up to Jesus after you have eaten. What would you say to him at that point? What might he say to you, especially in regard to your own times of concern and worry about your daily bread?

Conclude with an Our Father.

_____

_____

_____

_____

_____

_____

_____

_____

_____

_____

_____

_____

_____

_____

_____

_____

_____

_____

_____

_____

_____

_____

_____

The Effects of the Miracle

And they all ate and were satisfied. And they took up twelve baskets full of the broken pieces left over. And those who ate were about five thousand men, besides women and children. Then he made the disciples get into the boat and go before him to the other side, while he dismissed the crowds. (Matthew 14:20-22)

So abundant is this miracle that twelve baskets of fragments are collected. Still today, people in the Middle East become quite uncomfortable when they see a piece of bread lying on the ground or street. I have seen them pick it up, kiss it, and move it to a place where the birds can eat it without it being stepped on. Sometimes they gather large amounts of bread fragments to dry in the sun, and then they feed it to domestic animals rather than see it go to waste. Because bread is highly respected in that culture, the gathering of the fragments into baskets fits the people's mentality.

An interesting side point is that the Greek word for "basket" is *kophinoi*, a wide-weave basket such as would hold the large St. Peter's fish that are commonly caught on the west side of the lake. This differs from the term used in the second multiplication of loaves on the east side of the Sea of Galilee, where the fragments are gathered in *spuridas* (Mark 8:8), narrow-weave baskets more appropriate for the smaller sardines commonly caught on the northeastern side of the lake. This difference in terms indicates that the Evangelists faithfully recorded the traditions handed on to them, accurately reflecting the realities of fishing life on the Sea of Galilee.

Finally, Jesus sends the disciples away in the boat and dismisses the crowds so that he can accomplish his original goal: being alone with his Father in personal prayer. St. John adds that the crowd wanted to make him a king that would provide them with more bread, like the Roman emperor did ("Perceiving then that they were about to come and take him by force to make him king, Jesus withdrew again to the hills by himself" [6:15].) However, Jesus resists that temptation and goes off to pray before yet another adventure or miracle begins.

The conclusion of this miracle shows that Jesus' compassion for the crowd and his ability to meet their needs is paramount. He does not seek anything for himself, and he rejects their attempts to use his miraculous powers for their own economic and political needs.

When you look back on the wonderful ways in which God has provided for you in your need, do you keep your focus on his loving compassion, or does your attention slip toward a desire for him to keep on providing care? Does your focus remain on the Christ, the Giver and Source of the goodness we receive, or does it move to the gifts themselves? Stand with Christ as he goes off to enter a time of prayer with the Father and ask him how you have treated his gifts and him. Is there a need to return the focus on Jesus and the Father's providence? Do you need to repent of focusing on the gifts instead of the Giver? What are some of the specific circumstances in which you turned more to expecting the gifts or even demanding them rather than praising the Father who has given them?

Conclude with an Our Father.

_____

_____

_____

_____

_____

_____

_____

_____

_____

_____

_____

_____

_____

_____

_____

_____

_____

_____

CHAPTER 10

Walking on the Storms of Life

MATTHEW 14:23-33

Jesus Prays in Solitude
and Walks on Water

And after he had dismissed the crowds, he went into the hills
by himself to pray. When evening came, he was there alone, but
the boat by this time was many furlongs distant from the land,
beaten by the waves; for the wind was against them. And in the
fourth watch of the night he came to them, walking on the sea.
(Matthew 14:23-25)

Having healed and fed the large crowd that had followed
him to the place where he sought solitude after the
death of John the Baptist, Jesus sends both the disciples and the large crowd away. He could now be alone as he
had first intended. Nothing is said about what he did alone, but
based on previous passages, he used the occasion to commune
with his Father.

Not only was such time for private prayer necessary for Jesus
during his own mission, but it is also crucial for every Christian
disciple throughout their vocation and mission. Too frequently it
is said about many (though certainly not all) priests and religious
who leave their orders and ministry that they had stopped praying. And yet many who remain in the clerical or religious life have
survived great trials, difficulties, and even persecutions, sustained
through it all by prayer. This is also the case for those in families.
Time alone with God is the way to gain perspective on ourselves
as well as to discern the purpose and meaning of our lives and
activities and the next steps that God may want us to take.

From his place on the hill next to the Sea of Galilee, Jesus could see that the disciples in their boat were in serious trouble as another squall rose up during the night. Again the disciples were caught in this difficulty precisely because they had followed his instructions, so Jesus comes out to them, walking on the water.

While Christians are generally familiar with this scene of Jesus walking on the water, they rarely see it through an Old Testament lens. The psalmist writes, "Your way was through the sea, / your path through the great waters; / yet your footprints were unseen. / You led your people like a flock / by the hand of Moses and Aaron" (77:19-20). This psalm speaks about the Lord making his "way" or road through the sea and his path through the water, which is obviously a reference to leading the people of Israel through the Red Sea on their way out of Egypt. However, the Book of Job notes that God "alone . . . trampled the waves of the sea" (9:8). Clearly, in the Old Testament only the Lord God walks upon the waters of the sea. Here Jesus goes out to meet his disciples as they confront the winds and storm by doing what only God can do: walk upon the Sea of Galilee. His doing so will once again answer the important question of Jesus' identity.

In this scene we see two of the aspects of prayer: Jesus demonstrating his personal desire for a prayer of contemplation and union with the Father and the disciples in a very dangerous situation in which they need God's help. Jesus seeks the time of solitude in order to be close to the Father; people in distress, like the disciples here, feel alone and sometimes abandoned by God.

Think back on both types of your experience of God. When have you found the Lord closest to you? Was it on a retreat? A holy hour? Some other time alone? Picture yourself being with Jesus in his time of solitary prayer, and recall some of your own most memorable times alone with God. What would Jesus say to you about the importance of prayer in his ministry? What would you say to him about your own times of deep prayer? What might he say to you about your private prayer from his perspective?

Consider also those times of great difficulty in your life when you may have felt abandoned by God. Like the apostles in the boat, you may have experienced terrible problems precisely at times when you were doing exactly what God had asked of you. As you picture Jesus as he walks on the water, speak to him about those times when you felt lost or abandoned in the storms of life. What would you say to him? What might he say to you about those occasions from his perspective?

Conclude with the prayer the Soul of Christ.

_____

_____

_____

_____

_____

_____

_____

_____

_____

_____

_____

_____

_____

The Disciples in the Boat

But when the disciples saw him walking on the sea, they were
terrified, saying, "It is a ghost!" And they cried out for fear. But
immediately he spoke to them, saying, "Take heart, it is I; have
no fear." (Matthew 14:26-27)

By no means do the disciples grasp Jesus' identity yet. In
addition to their fears due to the strong storm and winds,
now they see Jesus walking on the sea and become terrified, crying aloud from fear. Their first explanation of this sight
is that they are seeing a ghost. This will be their "go-to" explanation yet again when Jesus enters the upper room on Easter
Sunday night: "But they were startled and frightened, and supposed that they saw a spirit" (Luke 24:37). In both situations,
the "ghost" explanation makes more sense to them than believ-
ing that they are seeing Jesus do what is otherwise impossible
by nature.

Jesus immediately addresses the terrified disciples in the boat
with three statements of encouragement. First, he tells them to
"take heart" and have courage. Obviously, Jesus needs to say
this to them because they are so frightened at this apparition
during a storm. Just because calling Jesus a ghost is their sim-
plest explanation, it does not mean that it is the most comforting
one. In a storm that already has them working hard to save their
lives, the appearance to all of them together of someone walking
on the water obviously terrifies them. Jesus calls them to take
courage and not let their fear overwhelm them.

Second, Jesus says to them, "It is I." Although this is the wording in the Revised Standard Version and other translations, the Greek text says simply, "I am." So as Jesus walks on the stormy waters, he identifies himself with the phrase "I am." This is the name God revealed to Moses at the burning bush (Exodus 3:14), a somewhat elusive name that both identifies the Lord God and maintains the mystery of his infinity. In this present context of walking on the water, which only the Lord God does in the Old Testament, Jesus' self-identification as "I am" becomes yet another indicator of his divine nature. He will frequently identify himself as "I am" in John's Gospel (8:24, 28, 58; 13:19; 18:5, 6, 8).

Third, Jesus says, "Have no fear," a command which is often addressed to individuals when they encounter God or his angels (Genesis 15:1; 46:3; Isaiah 41:10, 14; 43:1; 44:2; Luke 1:13, 30; Matthew 28:5; Acts 18:9-10; 27:24; Revelation 1:17). This again is a response to their obvious panic as they cry aloud in the stormy sea. However, Jesus' command is a response not only to the disciples' present danger but also to his divine presence. The greatness and immensity of God overwhelms those who experience it directly, and God needs to reassure the disciples that his divine presence walking upon the waves is not meant for their harm.

Imagine yourself being in the boat with the disciples as they see Jesus come to them walking on the water during the storm. Relate to their fright by going back to situations in your life when you were overwhelmed by fearful circumstances. Perhaps you even had a particularly frightening experience of God's presence in your life. Then focus on Jesus as he approaches the boat. What would his words mean to you? How would you react to hearing him say, "Take heart; have courage"? When you hear him say, "I am," what comes to your mind? How do you react to him identifying himself to you in this way? How do his words "Fear not" strike you at this point? Speak to him in the storm. What might he say to you now?

Conclude with the prayer the Soul of Christ.

_____

_____

_____

_____

_____

_____

_____

_____

_____

_____

_____

_____

_____

_____

_____

_____

_____

Peter Walks on the Waves

And Peter answered him, "Lord, if it is you, bid me come to you on the water." He said, "Come." So Peter got out of the boat and walked on the water and came to Jesus; but when he saw the wind, he was afraid, and beginning to sink he cried out, "Lord, save me." Jesus immediately reached out his hand and caught him, saying to him, "O man of little faith, why did you doubt?" And when they got into the boat, the wind ceased. And those in the boat worshiped him, saying, "Truly you are the Son of God." (Matthew 14:28-33)

Peter demonstrates an aspect of his leadership among the disciples by speaking to the presumed "ghost" with a challenge to present proof that it is really Jesus. His test for discerning the authenticity of Jesus' presence is based on his willingness to take a personal risk: "Bid me come to you." He does not suggest that anyone else take the risk of walking on the water to Jesus. He continues to demonstrate his leadership by following Jesus' command to come and actually getting out of the boat. Peter was no naive fool; he had been fishing on the Sea of Galilee for years, and he well knew that no one could walk on water, yet alone during a storm that aroused fear in well-experienced sailors. Yet he goes out and walks to Jesus!

Up to this point, Peter is doing fine, but as almost every preacher in history has noted, the problem comes when he takes his eyes off Jesus and focuses on the storm. Turning his attention to the danger instead of to Jesus, who not only walks above the danger but empowers him to do the same, causes Peter to sink. At Peter's cry for salvation, Jesus reaches out a hand to lift him up and then rebukes his lack of faith. Then, when Jesus gets into the boat, the wind and the storm cease. This, along with the walk on water, indicates Jesus divinity, since it is the Lord God who maintains such control over the wind and the sea. No wonder those in the boat "worshiped" him and said in faith that Jesus is truly "the Son of God"(Matthew 14:33).

On a certain level, the disciples come to a new level of faith in Jesus. Perhaps they have now attained a glimmer of understanding about Jesus' divinity from his divine act of walking on water and empowering Simon Peter to walk on water with him. They may even have an insight into Jesus' hint of a claim to be "I am." Such hints will grow and develop over time, but we can see them beginning to emerge at this point when Jesus comes out to meet them in their need.

Many Christians experience crises of faith similar to that of Peter walking on water when they are faced with life's problems and dangers. They easily become tempted to cry out, "Why is this happening to me?" or "Where is God?" or "Why doesn't God do something now when I need him?" Think back on your own life and the ways in which you may have acted like Peter walking on the crises and storms of your own life. Picture Jesus standing before you in those moments. How would you answer Jesus' question, "Why did you doubt?" If he called you a person of "little faith," what would you say to him? What would our Lord say to you?

Conclude with slowly praying the Our Father with Jesus.

_____

_____

_____

_____

_____

_____

_____

_____

_____

_____

_____

_____

_____

_____

_____

_____

_____

_____

_____

_____

_____

_____

CHAPTER 11

A Syrophoenician Woman

MATTHEW 15:21-28

A Syrophoenician Woman Approaches Jesus for an Exorcism

And Jesus went away from there and withdrew to the district of Tyre and Sidon. And behold, a Canaanite woman from that region came out and cried, "Have mercy on me, O Lord, Son of David; my daughter is severely possessed by a demon." (Matthew 15:21-22)

After a dispute with the Pharisees and scribes over the failure of Jesus' disciples to wash their hands when they eat and over the meaning of what is clean before God (see Matthew 15:1-20; Mark 7:1-23), Jesus and his disciples leave Jewish Galilee for the Gentile "district of Tyre and Sidon." These were ancient coastal cities that had dominated southern Lebanon. In going there, Jesus walks into territory that was considered religiously unclean by Jews.

St. Matthew often begins important events with the word "behold" in order to draw the reader's attention to something especially interesting. Here it is the unusual case of a Canaanite woman who approaches Jesus with a request for "mercy" because her daughter is possessed by a demon. Recall that the Canaanites had lived in the region before Abraham and the Israelite conquest. The Old Testament associated Canaanites with magical practices, orgiastic worship of Baal and Ashtarte, and child sacrifice. When the Israelites conquered them, it was viewed as a punishment from the Lord for these crimes.

However, this Canaanite woman shows persistent love of her daughter and faith in Jesus. Amazingly, she addresses Jesus as "Lord, Son of David." Calling him "Lord" indicates a faith by which she is willing to submit herself to him. While generally the title "Lord" could indicate the presence of an important person, it also opens itself to the deeper meaning of Jesus as Lord and God, which would be an astounding level of faith coming from a Canaanite. By calling him "Son of David," she may be appealing to the ancient and positive relationship between Hiram, king of Tyre, and David and his son Solomon (see 2 Samuel 5:11; 1 Kings 5:1-14).

Having addressed Jesus so positively, she petitions him, "Have mercy on me," because her daughter is "severely possessed by a demon." The word "severely" translates a Greek adverb, "evilly," which is used to show the intensity of the demon possession of the girl. None of the specific demonic action is described, but it is obvious that the girl suffers intensely and that the mother is greatly distressed by all that her daughter is enduring from this malevolent spirit.

This mother was overwhelmed by the evil that afflicted her daughter. Constantly in human history, evil has viciously attacked the weak and vulnerable. To many, this has been scandalous, and it has even led some to despair. Consider the attacks of evil forces against the young in the modern world: secular forces insist on the power to kill the unborn, and Islamists rape and kill young children. Child sexual abuse is rampant in some places; in other places, particularly in Africa, children are forced to join militias and fight in wars. Frequently the world ignores these evils, and some societies even justify them.

In the faces of these and other forces of evil in our world, imagine yourself as the Canaanite woman standing before Jesus.

With deep faith, profess Jesus as your Lord, as the Son of David who fulfills the promise of the Messiah from David's family. Ask him yet again to show his lordship over your life, and exercise the power that defeats the forces of sin and evil, first in your life and then in our society.

Conclude with an Our Father.

Jesus' Mission Determines His Response

But he did not answer her a word. And his disciples came and begged him, saying, "Send her away, for she is crying after us." He answered, "I was sent only to the lost sheep of the house of Israel." (Matthew 15:23-24)

Jesus does not respond at all but remains silent. The disciples plead with him, not because they care about the woman or her daughter's welfare, but because she is annoying them. They show neither love for the neighbor in need nor faith in Jesus' power to cure the demon-possessed daughter. They simply do not want to be bothered by her loud cries for help.

Jesus then speaks to the disciples, explaining his silence on the basis of the principle he had taught them when he sent them on their first mission: "Go nowhere among the Gentiles, and enter no town of the Samaritans, but go rather to the lost sheep of the house of Israel" (Matthew 10:5-6).

His mission to the lost sheep of Israel is rooted in the prophets rather than some personal animosity. Recall that after Judah's defeat and exile by the Babylonians, Jeremiah foretold that the people would say, "Come, let us join ourselves to the LORD in an everlasting covenant which will never be forgotten" (50:5). They had broken the covenant, and as the Lord had warned, they had lost their land. Yet the Lord was willing to receive them back, saying through Jeremiah, "My people have been lost sheep; their shepherds have led them astray" (50:6). Jesus had come to give them the "new covenant in [his] blood" (Luke 22:20; cf. Matthew 26:28; Mark 14:24); he had come to the people with whom the Lord had made the covenants with Abraham and Moses and to whom the Lord had promised a new covenant. As the prophet Jeremiah had prophesied, "Behold, the days are coming, says the LORD, when I will make a new covenant with the house of Israel and the house of Judah" (31:31).

Such was Jesus' mission, to which he was simply being faithful. He did not reject the people outside of Israel, nor did he dislike them. Rather, the mission to Israel came first, and the mission to the Gentiles would remain at a later stage after his resurrection and ascension and Pentecost.

We must deal with two problems in this section of the passage. First, we do not want to be like the disciples who simply want to avoid the inconvenience of listening to the woman's loud and repeated cries for help. With so many attacks of evil in our world, we can be overwhelmed and try to shut out the cries of other people. To avoid such coldness, we need to be with Jesus, not like the apostles in this moment. We need to have an attentiveness to him and his mission. Silence with him and a willingness to continue to love God and neighbor will open our hearts and minds to a readiness to act on the mission that Jesus wants to give us. This may not be the first need we perceive but the deeper mission in which we have a unique role to play that others cannot accomplish in the way that God wants it done.

Second, we need to listen to Jesus explain his mission for the world. Both a peace that comes from careful attentiveness to Jesus and an urgency inspired by the needs of the world are kept in tension and balance as we move forward along the mission. This mission is not merely some human enterprise but a call from God to accomplish his plan in the world. In accepting that call, we move to a deeper level of accepting his lordship over our lives.

Spend some time in silence with the Lord. Ask him to open your heart to love him and your neighbor. Listen to Jesus explain his mission for the world. What does he want you to do? Where does he want you to begin?

Conclude with an Our Father.

_____

_____

_____

_____

_____

_____

_____

_____

_____

_____

_____

_____

_____

_____

_____

_____

_____

_____

Humble Wisdom Wins an Answer

But she came and knelt before him, saying, "Lord, help me."
And he answered, "It is not fair to take the children's bread
and throw it to the dogs." She said, "Yes, Lord, yet even the
dogs eat the crumbs that fall from their master's table." Then
Jesus answered her, "O woman, great is your faith! Be it done
for you as you desire." And her daughter was healed instantly.
(Matthew 15:25-28)

The distressed woman kneels before Jesus, a posture of
petition, and renews her plea for help directly in front of
him. Rather than using a direct yes or no, Jesus responds
in a proverbial style, using an everyday image of taking bread
from children, the dependent members of the family, and giving
it to the dogs, who were not part of the family. Jews considered dogs to be unclean animals, not the highly regarded pets of
the wealthy modern world. Shepherds might have dogs, but not
many people, especially not the poor, kept them as pets in Israel.
Some pagan societies, such as that of the Canaanite woman, did
not consider dogs unclean and might have been more familiar
with them. Jesus here uses an image that she might well understand less offensively than a Jewish audience would.

In response, the woman answers with another proverbial
statement about the inevitable crumbs that fall from the table
when children are eating. The dogs may not be permitted to
take the children's portion of the food, but they happily sit near
the table to eat whatever may fall to them. She expresses great

humility in making this comparison to her request. She has some understanding of Jesus' primary mission to the "lost sheep of the house of Israel" (Matthew 15:24), and she is eager to accept any crumbs of his power that may fall to her. Her daughter is healed instantly.

In her very humble answer, Jesus recognizes authentic faith. Her combination of wisdom and humility shows that she is ready to receive his salvation, as was the case with the wisdom and humility of the centurion, who knew he was unworthy to have Jesus under his roof (Matthew 8:8).

This interchange teaches us the importance of wisdom and humility. Wisdom prevents wickedness from prevailing over goodness: "Against wisdom evil does not prevail" (Wisdom 7:30). In this case, the woman's wisdom drew on the goodness of Christ to defeat the evil spirit that possessed her daughter.

The power of humility in prayer is a frequent theme in the wisdom literature of Scripture:

Toward the scorners he is scornful, / but to the humble he shows favor. (Proverbs 3:34)

When pride comes, then comes disgrace; / but with the humble is wisdom. (Proverbs 11:2)

Those who fear the Lord will prepare their hearts, / and will humble themselves before him. (Sirach 2:17)

For great is the might of the Lord; / he is glorified by the humble. (Sirach 3:20)

The prayer of the humble pierces the clouds, / and he will not be consoled until it reaches the Lord; / he will not desist until the

Most High visits him, / and does justice for the righteous, and executes judgment. (Sirach 35:17)

We would do well to consider the need for both of these qualities in our own lives. Wisdom not only comes from God but Jesus personifies wisdom; he is "our wisdom, our righteousness and sanctification and redemption" (1 Corinthians 1:30). Rather than demanding an answer, the Syrophoenician woman recognizes the truth of what Jesus, the Son of David, tells her. She shows wisdom with her insightful observation of dogs eating the scraps that fall from the table. By this she humbly expresses her willingness to accept the scraps because that would be sufficient to free her daughter from evil.

How do we acquire these virtues? Picture yourself standing next to Jesus after he pronounces the cure of the woman's daughter. Speak to him about her virtues of wisdom and humility and where they come from. Humility is not about putting oneself down since that continues the focus on oneself, only without boasting. Humility is the focus on God's greatness that gives lowly human beings perspective on how weak, ignorant, and sinful they actually are. His greatness does not disdain our smallness but cherishes us when we accept ourselves the way he does—with great love for who and what we are, with a willingness to become more like him and receive from him.

Wisdom is not the same as great learning; neither is it about acquiring all the facts in the world. People who know a lot of information may still be very foolish. Rather, it is the ability to reflect on the information we have and make sense of life in correspondence to the truth of what exists. Wisdom does not make life correspond to our theories but rather has the humility to let our theories correspond to reality. God is the great source of wisdom, for which reason we can say, "Fear of the LORD is the beginning of wisdom" (Psalm 111:10; cf. Proverbs 1:7).

Ask Jesus to know him even more so that you might acquire his perspective on you, the view that is the source of true humility and wisdom. Ask him for the patience to observe yourself, life in this world, and his teaching in Scripture and the Church so as to acquire the wisdom that he gives and that he is.

Conclude with the prayer the Soul of Christ.

CHAPTER 12

Jesus Heals a Deaf Man

MARK 7:31-37

Opening Ears and Mouth

Then he returned from the region of Tyre, and went through
Sidon to the Sea of Galilee, through the region of the Decapolis.
And they brought to him a man who was deaf and had an impediment in his speech; and they besought him to lay his hand upon
him. And taking him aside from the multitude privately, he put
his fingers into his ears, and he spat and touched his tongue; and
looking up to heaven, he sighed, and said to him, "Ephphatha,"
that is, "Be opened." And his ears were opened, his tongue was
released, and he spoke plainly. (Mark 7:31-35)

Jesus has left Jewish territory after a dispute with the Pharisees over the meaning of being truly clean (see Matthew
15:1-20; Mark 7:1-23). First he goes to the region of Tyre
and Sidon, which is southern Lebanon today, and there exor-
cizes the demon from a woman's daughter. Then he makes a
roundabout journey from southern Lebanon to the Decapolis,
a region of ten Gentile cities east of the Sea of Galilee located
in modern Syria and Jordan. This journey allows Jesus to avoid
Jewish territory, which may have been his intention because of
the opposition he faced from Herod and the Pharisees. Jesus
has already demonstrated his authority in this district by cast-
ing the legion of demons out of a man (Mark 5:1-20) and the
demon from the little girl (Matthew 15:21-28), and now he will
continue to show his authority in Gentile territory when people bring him a deaf man with a speech impediment. They show
faith in Jesus by asking him to lay hands on the man.

However, Jesus does not follow the crowd's suggestion of simply laying hands on the man. First, he takes the deaf man aside, away from the crowd, so that he can heal without being a showman who seeks to draw people's attention to himself for his own benefit. Jesus is concerned about the person in need and not with advancing his reputation.

Second, he acts far more intimately and symbolically than just laying hands on him. He puts his fingers into the man's two ears and touches his tongue. He even places spittle from his own mouth onto the tongue of the man who has difficulty in speaking as a type of sacramental for healing, similar to the disciples' use of oil during their mission (Mark 6:13). However, rather than using oil from olive trees, he uses his own spittle for a more intimate connection with the man.

Third, he prays. He looks up to heaven, a sign by which he recognizes that the healing originates with his Father. Mark then says he "sighed" or "groaned," a term used for childbirth (Jeremiah 4:31), mortal combat (Ezekiel 24:17), and Job's suffering (23:2). The psalms frequently use forms of this root word in its prayers, especially in laments (see Psalms 6:7; 30:11; 37:9), which are the most likely background for Jesus' prayer here.

Finally, Jesus says, "Be opened." St. Mark gives the transliteration of the Aramaic "Ephphatha," because readers in the Hellenistic world liked miracle stories with foreign words in it. It is worth noting that the only place in the Old Testament that mentions the healing of a speech impediment is the prophecy of the end times in Isaiah 35:5: "Then the eyes of the blind shall be opened, / and the ears of the deaf unstopped." Clearly Jesus is fulfilling this verse among these Gentiles by healing their deaf neighbor.

Part of the Rite of Baptism of children is the "Ephphatha," in which the priest places his fingers on the ears and tongue of the candidate, not as a prayer for a physical healing, but that the Lord Jesus might soon touch the child's ears to receive God's word and his mouth to proclaim the faith. As one of the baptized now mature enough to read these words yourself, picture yourself in private with Jesus and ask him to place his fingers on your ears and mouth. Ask him to open your ears to hear the word of God in Sacred Scripture, Sacred Tradition, and the Church's magisterium ever more deeply so that his word would enter your soul with greater understanding. Ask him to touch your mouth so that you might speak his word ever more clearly, spreading it among the people around you.

Then speak to him about those things that might still be blocking you from hearing his word. What holds you back from being able to listen to him speak to you through his word? What holds you back from speaking his word to others? What would Jesus say to you about either side of this equation? What would you say to him?

Conclude with the prayer the Soul of Christ.

_____

_____

_____

_____

_____

_____

_____

The Secrecy of Jesus' Mission

And he charged them to tell no one; but the more he charged them, the more zealously they proclaimed it. And they were astonished beyond measure, saying, "He has done all things well; he even makes the deaf hear and the dumb speak." (Mark 7:36-37)

As was true after the healing of the leper in Mark 1:40-45, so here Jesus orders the people to keep the miracle to themselves and tell no one. There are two aspects to Jesus' insistence on secrecy in regard to his great works. First, we read a comment in Matthew, which is a quotation from Isaiah 42:1-4 about the nature of the Messiah that Isaiah foretold and Jesus fulfilled:

This was to fulfil what was spoken by the prophet Isaiah: Behold, my servant whom I have chosen, / my beloved with whom my soul is well pleased. / I will put my Spirit upon him, / and he shall proclaim justice to the Gentiles. / He will not wrangle or cry aloud, / nor will any one hear his voice in the streets; / he will not break a bruised reed / or quench a smoldering wick, / till he brings justice to victory; / and in his name will the Gentiles hope. (Matthew 12:17-21)

After the fact of the miracle, Jesus does not want notoriety that puts the attention on him as a wonder worker; rather, he truly is humble and meek, the One to whom we all should come: "Take my yoke upon you, and learn from me; for I am gentle and lowly in heart, and you will find rest for your souls" (Matthew 11:29).

Second, Jesus silences those who witness his miracles because being the Messiah is not primarily connected with accomplishing miracles. Certainly we have seen that the miracles have raised the question of his identity for the apostles, especially when he calmed the storm and walked on the water. Yet his role as the Messiah and Son of God cannot be fully understood in the healings and other miracles. Nor can the recognition of his being the Son of God be understood in light of the exorcisms. He silences everyone who calls him the Son of God, and he commands people to be silent about his miracles throughout the Gospel, with one exception. After he has died on the cross, the centurion proclaims, "Truly this was the Son of God" (Matthew 27:54; cf. Mark 15:39). The secret of Jesus' divinity can be made known at the cross because his death is the core of the true meaning of being the Messiah. Healing the deaf and mute man is good, but it is not the essence of salvation. Jesus' mission, the reason for which he was sent, is his death on the cross and his glorious resurrection, and he wants us to stay focused on that reality.

Speak to Jesus about his humility in regard to his performing miracles and healing. What might he say to you about the way in which he humbly and quietly accomplishes his mission? How might his words and attitude be a challenge to the way you live out the specific tasks of your mission to preach the gospel and do the good that he asks of you?

Then speak to him about the priorities of his mission. Ask him to deepen your understanding of the priority of the cross and the salvation he has won for the human race by dying for our sins. Speak to him about the role of the miracles and exorcisms within the context of his mission to redeem sinners from the cross.

Conclude with the prayer the Soul of Christ.

_____

_____

_____

_____

_____

_____

_____

_____

_____

_____

_____

_____

_____

_____

_____

_____

_____

_____

_____

_____

_____

CHAPTER 13

Sailing to Bethsaida

MARK 8:11-21

The Demand for a Sign

The Pharisees came and began to argue with him, seeking from him a sign from heaven, to test him. And he sighed deeply in his spirit, and said, "Why does this generation seek a sign? Truly, I say to you, no sign shall be given to this generation." (Mark 8:11-12)

The Pharisees approach Jesus as soon as he gets off the boat and lands in Dalmanutha. This is consistent with their earlier confrontations with Jesus when they challenged his authority to forgive sins (Mark 2:6-7) and when he ate with sinners (2:16), let the disciples pluck grain on the Sabbath (2:23-24), healed on the Sabbath (3:4-6), cast out of demons (3:22), and allowed the disciples to eat with unwashed hands (7:1ff). Now their dispute concerns proof by a sign from God that he has authority to preach and do miracles and eat bread and fish among the Gentiles, who were considered unclean people. The very series of Jesus' successful ministries among the Gentiles has now become the reason to challenge him.

The Pharisees seek a sign from Jesus—not a miracle, but a sign "from heaven," that is, from God himself, affirming Jesus and his ministry, particularly to the Gentiles. They have witnessed miracles, but those are not the authenticating sign they want.

Jesus "sighed deeply in his spirit," such as Ezekiel did before pronouncing a judgment:

"Sigh therefore, son of man; sigh with breaking heart and bitter grief before their eyes. And when they say to you, 'Why do you sigh?' you shall say, 'Because of the tidings. When it comes, every heart will melt and all hands will be feeble, every spirit will faint and all knees will be weak as water. Behold, it comes and it will be fulfilled,'" says the Lord GOD. (Ezekiel 21:6-7)

Then he asks rhetorically why "this generation" seeks a sign. Note that Genesis 7:1 refers to the people about to be destroyed in the flood as "this generation," while Psalm 95:10 says, "For forty years I loathed that generation / and said, 'They are a people who err in heart, / and they do not regard my ways.'" Jesus' deep sigh is a preparation for a judgment against the people questioning him.

He answers in an Aramaic or Hebrew idiomatic expression, as seen in this literal translation of the Greek words: "Amen I say to you, if a sign will be given to this generation." This is reminiscent of Psalm 95:11: "Therefore I swore in my anger / that they should not enter my rest." Literally, this is translated as "if they enter into my rest." This is a type of oath formula that leaves the consequences unstated and implies, in Jesus' statement here, a threat. If that generation did receive a sign, the sign might be a great punishment, such as the threat about the end of the world or the destruction of Jerusalem in Mark 13.

At their core, the Pharisees lack faith to see that Jesus' miracles are truly signs that fulfill the Old Testament promises about the Messiah and his times. The healings, exorcisms, and multiplication of bread and fish, both among the Jews and among the Gentiles, point to him being the Messiah. However, without faith no sign will ever satisfy, and that is the condition Jesus finds among these Pharisees. Their rejection incites him to make his final crossing of the Sea of Galilee that will mark the end of the Galilean mission and the beginning of a new stage of teaching his disciples on the way to Jerusalem.

Consider that the Pharisees ask Jesus for a sign in order to "test him." They set themselves up as his judges, and he refuses to accept that role from them. Throughout the Gospels, he identifies himself as "the Son of man," a reference to the judge at the end of time:

> I saw in the night visions, and behold, with the clouds of heaven / there came one like a son of man, / and he came to the Ancient of Days / and was presented before him. (Daniel 7:13)

> Then I looked, and lo, a white cloud, and seated on the cloud one like a son of man, with a golden crown on his head, and a sharp sickle in his hand. (Revelation 14:14)

Jesus will be the one to test their deeds and judge them; he will himself be the sign when he comes on the clouds to judge the living and the dead.

Picture yourself standing next to Jesus as he answers the Pharisees. Speak to him of times when your faith has been tempted and you wanted some proof from him that he is real. Speak to him of the circumstances that raised such questions for you. Ask him what he thinks about the kinds of tests or the search for signs that you have made in his regard. What might he say to you, especially in reflection on how your faith has developed since that time?

Conclude with the prayer the Soul of Christ.

_____

_____

_____

_____

_____

_____

_____

_____

_____

_____

_____

_____

_____

_____

_____

_____

_____

_____

_____

_____

_____

_____

The Blindness of the Disciples

And he left them, and getting into the boat again he departed to the other side. Now they had forgotten to bring bread; and they had only one loaf with them in the boat. And he cautioned them, saying, "Take heed, beware of the leaven of the Pharisees and the leaven of Herod." And they discussed it with one another, saying, "We have no bread." (Mark 8:13-16)

Mark tells us readers that the disciples had forgotten to bring loaves and had only one loaf with them in the boat. This description of one problem becomes the background for another problem: the disciples' misunderstanding of Jesus' saying about the "leaven of the Pharisees" (Mark 8:15). The disciples focus on their lack of bread, perhaps out of their need for bread to give them energy to row across the lake. They may have thought about how they would have to break the bread into thirteen pieces, allowing each of them to have only a little bit that would leave them unsatisfied. With such a focus, they would blame themselves—or more likely each other—for their failure to bring along enough bread. Their focus on the lack of loaves and the presence of "one loaf" at the same time diverts their attention from Jesus, the Bread of Life, who is present in the boat.

At this point, Jesus warns them, "Beware of the leaven of the Pharisees and the leaven of Herod" (Mark 8:15). All they can hear is a reminder of their lack of loaves. Jesus has in mind his recent encounter with the Pharisees (8:11-12), who tested him by demanding a sign, which he refused to give. Here Jesus warns the disciples against the leaven, that is, the influence of the Pharisees and Herod. Herod was someone who had heard of Jesus but interpreted him through the prism of his own deeds, specifically the killing of John the Baptist (see 6:14-29). The Herodians plotted to kill Jesus after he had healed a man in a synagogue on the Sabbath (3:6), and they would later try to entrap him by asking about paying taxes to Caesar (12:13-17; Matthew 22:16-21). Jesus' warning against the leaven of the Herodians is concerned with political forces that could easily divert them from keeping the kingdom of God primary in their lives.

The disciples misunderstand Jesus' words about leaven, and they only think about their lack of bread. They reduce Christ's warning from one of concern for the bad influences of the Pharisees and the Herodians to their desire for more loaves of bread. Their practical and simple perspective blocks out the very important truths that Jesus has spoken to them.

We would do well to examine our own consciences to better understand where we have placed our focus of attention. Picture yourself in the boat with Jesus on this final crossing of the Sea of Galilee during his earthly mission, and consider the following questions in his presence. Do you concern yourself with the lack of things in life, or focus on the things you actually do possess, missing the presence of Jesus Christ in your midst? Are your prayers so focused on making sure you have material things that you neglect to spend time focused on the presence of Jesus in the tabernacles of your church? When you attend Mass, are you so attentive to the need to get out of the church parking lot ahead of everyone else that you fail to pay attention to Jesus, the Bread of Life, whom you have just received in Holy Communion? Speak to him of the ways in which you have misplaced your focus and attention, and listen to what he might say to you.

Conclude with the prayer the Soul of Christ.

_____

_____

_____

_____

_____

_____

_____

_____

_____

_____

_____

_____

_____

_____

_____

_____

_____

_____

_____

_____

_____

_____

_____

Jesus Confronts the Disciples' Lack of Understanding

And being aware of it, Jesus said to them, "Why do you discuss the fact that you have no bread? Do you not yet perceive or understand? Are your hearts hardened? Having eyes do you not see, and having ears do you not hear? And do you not remember? When I broke the five loaves for the five thousand, how many baskets full of broken pieces did you take up?" They said to him, "Twelve." "And the seven for the four thousand, how many baskets full of broken pieces did you take up?" And they said to him, "Seven." And he said to them, "Do you not yet understand?" (Mark 8:17-21)

Through a series of rhetorical questions, Jesus moves from their misplaced discussion about the lack of bread to their lack of comprehension of his teaching about the influence of those who do not believe and those who seek only political power. Their inability to understand is reinforced by blindness, deafness, and hardness of heart, which were the words Jesus used for those without faith in him:

> "And he said to them, 'To you has been given the secret of the kingdom of God, but for those outside everything is in parables; so that they may indeed see but not perceive, and may indeed hear but not understand; lest they should turn again, and be forgiven.'" Mark 4:11-12)

Despite having been given the "secret of the kingdom of God," the disciples remain unable to see or hear what Jesus is doing. This opens the possibility that their hearts are hardened, as Mark notes after Jesus walks on the water:

> When they saw him walking on the sea they thought it was a ghost, and cried out; for they all saw him, and were terrified. But immediately he spoke to them and said, "Take heart, it is I; have no fear." And he got into the boat with them and the wind ceased. And they were utterly astounded, for they did not understand about the loaves, but their hearts were hardened. (Mark 6:49-52)

Jesus' questions require them to state the numbers of baskets of leftover bread after each of the two miracles of the multiplication of the fish and loaves; they must repeat the symbolic numbers twelve and seven. However, Jesus asks rhetorically, "Do you not yet understand?" as a rebuke of them. Obviously they do not. This will have serious consequences if they do not repent and come to that deeper faith that understands Jesus. Ultimately, it will not be the miracles but Jesus' death on the cross that will clarify who he really is: the Christ, the Son of God proclaimed at the beginning of the Gospel of Mark (1:1).

Place yourself with the disciples as they row and sail across the Sea of Galilee with Jesus, consumed with their own thoughts of eating and keeping up their strength for this arduous work. Consider the various issues that might be on your mind: your work, salary, house and car payments, tuition, children, spouse, the respect you receive from peers and superiors. Consider the ways in which these concerns come to the forefront of your attention, while the readings at Mass, a sermon, or other prayers are a background within which you think about your concerns. Then consider Jesus' rebuke for relegating the importance of his words to background noise as you consider your own worries, anxieties, and interests. Which might he say to you about what you should truly fear, namely, those whose lack of faith in him makes him irrelevant? What might he say about placing political allegiances as a higher priority in "the real world" than his words and teachings? What would you say in response to Jesus about your issues and his?

Conclude with an Our Father.

_____

_____

_____

_____

_____

_____

_____

_____

_____

_____

_____

_____

_____

_____

_____

_____

_____

_____

_____

_____

Appendix

The Soul of Christ (Anima Christi)

Soul of Christ, sanctify me.
Body of Christ, save me.
Blood of Christ, inebriate me.
Water from the side of Christ, wash me.
Passion of Christ, strengthen me.
O good Jesus, hear me.
Within your wounds, hide me.
Let me never be separated from you.
From the wicked foe, defend me.
At the hour of my death, call me and bid me come to you,
So that with your angels and saints I may praise you
For all eternity.

the WORD
among us ®
The *Spirit* of Catholic Living

T his book was published by The Word Among Us. Since 1981, The Word Among Us has been answering the call of the Second Vatican Council to help Catholic laypeople encounter Christ in the Scriptures.

The name of our company comes from the prologue to the Gospel of John and reflects the vision and purpose of all of our publications: to be an instrument of the Spirit, whose desire is to manifest Jesus' presence in and to the children of God. In this way, we hope to contribute to the Church's ongoing mission of proclaiming the gospel to the world so that all people would know the love and mercy of our Lord and grow more deeply in their faith as missionary disciples.

Our monthly devotional magazine, *The Word Among Us*, features meditations on the daily and Sunday Mass readings, and currently reaches more than one million Catholics in North America and another half million Catholics in one hundred countries around the world. Our book division, The Word Among Us Press, publishes numerous books, Bible studies, and pamphlets that help Catholics grow in their faith.

To learn more about who we are and what we publish, log on to our website at www.wau.org. There you will find a variety of Catholic resources that will help you grow in your faith.

Embrace His Word, Listen to God . . .

www.wau.org